JOHN L. STODDARD'S LECTURES

JAPAN I   JAPAN II

CHINA

JOHN L. STODDARD'S LECTURES

ILLUSTRATED AND EMBELLISHED WITH VIEWS OF THE
WORLD'S FAMOUS PLACES AND PEOPLE, BEING
THE IDENTICAL DISCOURSES DELIVERED
DURING THE PAST EIGHTEEN
YEARS UNDER THE TITLE
OF THE STODDARD
LECTURES

COMPLETE IN TEN VOLUMES

VOL. III

BOSTON
BALCH BROTHERS CO.
MDCCCXCIX

JAPAN

I

LECTURE I

IT is now nearly four hundred years since the brave dis-
coverer, Magellan, first sailed around the world. Yet, till
comparatively recent times, three years were necessary
to complete the circuit. To-day,
some Phineas Fogg can put a girdle
round the earth in less than eighty
days, and messages are flashed to
us from China and Ceylon in less
than eighty seconds. The old-time
spirit of adventure amid unknown
scenes, which thrilled the traveler
of former years, has, therefore,
well-nigh disappeared. Of all
the surface of our globe, the
Polar Seas alone still bid defi-
ance to the approach of man;
though every year the ultimate
capitulation of those ice-bound
areas, lit by the aurora, becomes less remote.

EMPEROR.

The broad Atlantic has now
dwindled to an ocean ferry. Europe is measured, not by
weeks, but by hours. Constantinople, once so remotely Oriental, is but five days from London,—Cairo only six. Even

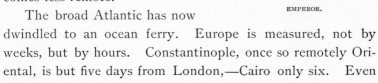

the vast Pacific glides beneath our keel in thirteen days.
Two centuries ago, the man who had achieved a journey
around the globe would have been called a hero.   One century since, he would have
been remarkable.   To-day
the name he earns is
merely—"Globe-trotter."
In consequence of this, to
certain minds our van-
quished earth seems like
a squeezed and juiceless
orange.   Material forces
have deprived it of ro-
mance, as age has robbed
the moon of atmosphere

MOUNT STEPHEN.

and life.   And yet, the fact that we move rapidly from point
to point need not lessen our interest in the places that we
visit.   The wondrous beauty of the Taj Mahal and the
incomparable majesty of the Himalayas are not less enjoyed
because we can make a pilgrimage to them with comparative
comfort.   Japan's awakened empire, China's four hundred
millions, the toiling myriads of India, with history, customs
and religions antedating those of Christendom, present the
same stupendous problems, whether we visit them in an
antique sailing-craft or in a modern steamer.   Despite the speed
with which we flit from continent to continent, the actual
distance is still there.   Let but the steamer's shaft become
disabled in mid-ocean, and the fact will not be doubted.   But
of whatever size our earth may now appear to us, the time
has never been when travel upon its surface offered such attractions.   Its countries now are like a series of intensely interesting books—each the sequel of its predecessor—which
science, commerce, and navigation have laid open for our
scrutiny.

A tour around the world, therefore, is vastly more instructive than a journey through the principal European cities. Mere Occidental travel, though delightful, is but fragmentary and one-sided. The unbroken circle is alone the symbol of completeness; and only when the traveler has sailed away from our Pacific coast, and journeyed on and on toward the setting sun, until he sees the shores of our Republic (never before so beloved) rise from the waves of the Atlantic, can he in truth exclaim, with Monte Cristo, "The world is mine!"

The route which we selected for our journey to Japan was the superbly built and admirably equipped highway to the Orient, the "Canadian Pacific." This magnificent transcontinental system comprises, first, the gleaming path of steel which crosses Canada from sea to sea; and, second, a fleet of steamers at the western terminus of the road—the largest, swiftest, and most modern boats that ply between the North American continent and the land of the Mikado. The various railway lines from the Atlantic to the centre of the continent are too well known to require description; but since some starting-point is necessary, we may well choose, as the most appropriate one, the vast plains of Manitoba, midway between the Atlantic and Pacific, and only eighteen hours by rail from Minneapolis. Mile after mile, and hour after hour, we sped through these prairies

A JAPANESE PAGODA.

as level as a tranquil sea.   Sometimes, like wreckage floating on the waves, we saw great sun-bleached heaps of skulls and bones—pathetic relics of the herds of buffaloes which only thirty years ago existed here in millions, but which man's cruelty and recklessness have almost totally destroyed.   At

other times, the railroad cut its silvery fur-row through a boundless area of goldenrod and daisies,— apparently a shoreless ocean of red, green, and gold, upon the verge of which the sky seemed to rest like an azure dome.   But presently we realized that the plains were being left be-hind us.   In fact, between these prairies and the vast

BANFF.

Pacific rise three great mountain-ranges almost parallel to one another.   They are the Rocky, the Selkirk, and the Cascade mountains.

It was already evening when we approached the "Rockies." We tried to catch their outline, but in vain.   Behind a

ON THE PORCH AT BANFF.

veil of impenetrable gloom, the morrow's splendid spectacle
awaited us. Accordingly, at five o'clock in the morning, the
subtle nervousness which usually heralds any long anticipated
pleasure woke me with a start. I raised the curtain of my
berth, and from my lips there came an exclamation of delight.
There were the "Rockies," as I had so often pictured them;
no longer vague creations of some other man's enthusiasm, but

A VIEW FROM THE HOTEL.

glorious realities awakening mine. A rugged wall of granite
met my gaze, seamed here and there with silver, as the pure
snow sparkled in its crevices; while all along its crest, five
thousand feet above our heads, the dawn had traced a
parapet of gold. I felt at once that thrill of satisfaction
which every traveler prizes more and more as years roll on
and fewer famous sights are left him to explore. It was
the consciousness of one more conquest made, not merely
for the excitement of a first possession, but for the calmer
and more abiding pleasure of retrospection.

An hour later, we had left the train to spend two days at
Banff,—a place unknown before the advent of the railroad,
but forming now the centre of a charming region, four thousand five hundred feet above the sea, reserved by the Canadian
Government as a national park. Above us, in the morning
light, like some old Rhenish castle on a wooded cliff, appeared
a picturesque hotel, within whose ample hall we found a

THE THREE SISTERS.

huge log blazing in the fireplace; while modern luxuries, such
as bath-rooms and electric-lights, assured us a delightful
resting-place. Yet this is but one of several hotels built by
the railroad company at points of special interest, so that the
traveler by this route may halt and view its scenery amid
comfortable surroundings.

Soon after our arrival, we started on a tour of exploration,
and found the situation worthy of its fame. Over the best
of roads Canadian ponies whirled us along the windings of
the Bow river, green as emerald. The air was as pure as

VANCOUVER.

that of Norway. A breath of it was like a draught of wine. So transparent was the atmosphere, that mountains miles away seemed close at hand. Strange mountains these! Their color is an ashen gray, now darkened by a passing cloud, now almost white with vivid sunlight. They have no vegetation on their rugged slopes, save a few pine-trees, which suggest the "forlorn hope" of an army struggling toward a citadel.

HOTEL VANCOUVER.

Had time permitted, we should have gladly lingered in this glorious region,—but with so much before us, we were compelled to take our leave of Banff and enter on the last great section of our journey toward the sea. In making this, we were for hours surfeited with grandeur. Our chief desire was to retard the train, and check the rapid shifting of imposing scenery. Our brains at last refused to receive additional impressions. One could spend weeks upon this portion of the route alone. Sometimes our train wound like a serpent around the mountain sides,—now on a narrow ledge three hundred feet above a foaming torrent, now gliding through a tunnel in the solid rock. Three million dollars' worth of snow-sheds guard this railway from the avalanche, and rivers even have been forced to turn aside and yield their immemorial pathways to the iron conqueror.

But now farewell to railroads and to mountains! We have reached the sea. Who that has ever crossed our mighty continent can quite forget the moment when, after all the plains and mountains he has traversed, he gains his first glimpse of the blue Pacific? It is at once a startling revelation of the distance he has come, and a reminder of

those Orient lands whose misty shores still seem so fabu-
lously far away.

Our ocean gateway, and place of embarkation for Japan,
was Vancouver,—one of those marvels of the West, which,
notwithstanding all our previous reading, astonish us when
actually seen.   Ten years ago Vancouver was a wilderness;
a forest covered every portion of the present city.   To-day
it has good streets and sidewalks, electric lights and trolley-
cars, banks, churches, some extremely pretty houses, and a good hotel.

THE EMPRESS OF JAPAN.

What an ex-
citement marks
the embarkation-
day at this Ho-
tel Vancouver!
What searching
glances pass from
one strange
group of travel-
ers to another, as if to read the characters and dispositions of
the men and women who are to be their fellow-passengers
for fourteen days,—aye, more than that;—to be, perchance,
their fellow-travelers for many months, meeting on other
steamers, or in Chinese streets, or possibly in the palm-groves
of Ceylon.   No gaiety is yet discernible.   It is the hour for
farewells.   The reading-room is filled with busy scribes, whose
scratching pens and long-drawn sighs alone disturb the silence
of the place.

We saw, on the last day, at least a score of ladies, bent
almost double on divans or arm-chairs, using alternately
their writing-tablets and their handkerchiefs,— their tears

THE "EMPRESS" IN A STORM.

apparently flowing much more freely than the ink from their fountain pens. Telegraph boys were meanwhile running to the various rooms with good-bye messages from eastern friends. "No use in sending them out," the *blasé* operator told me; "they are all alike. Might just as well hoist a flag with the letters 'B. V.' on it; for every message ends with the same words: 'Bon Voyage!'"

But now the actual sailing-time has come; the last fond messages have been received; the gang-plank is thrown off; the huge propeller moves; and we have left our native land

A JAPANESE VILLAGE.

to make the circuit of the world. Of course some tears are shed; some cheeks grow paler at the thought of all that lies before us in the twenty - five thousand miles of land and water we must traverse; but these are soon forgotten in contemplation of the ship itself,—the Empress of Japan. This is one of the finest steamers in the world, and like her sister ships, the Empress of China and the Empress of India, is a vessel of six thousand tons and of ten thousand horse-power. Graceful and beautiful she looked,—her great hull snow-white to the water's edge, to shield it better from the tropic sun.

Aside, however, from the speed, strength, and comfort of the steamers, the voyage across the North Pacific does not

call forth enthusiastic praise. It is a lonely, unfrequented
route. We saw no sign of land or life for thirteen days.
The cold, too, was excessive. Unless wrapped up with extra

MISSISSIPPI BAY.

care, we could
not sit on deck
with any com-
fort, although
protected from
the wind by
canvas screens.
Moreover, in its
sudden changes,
this North Pa-
cific rivals the
Mediterranean
in winter, and
when aroused, its billows are colossal. During our voyage
there were some hours, and even days, when all was reason-
ably calm; but there were others when tremendous winds
tore into shreds the crests of white-capped waves and filled
the air with blinding spray. Hours there were, when trunks
not merely slid, but bounded, clear across the room, and
landed with their casters in the air, like the hoofs of a rolling horse; hours when even the pantry stove revolted at such
treatment and hurled its glowing coals about the floor. I recall an unusually stormy period when the diet of at least two
wretched passengers for an entire day consisted of one grape,
—and my companion ate the grape!

The day which passed most quickly on this voyage was
that which we deliberately dropped from the calendar, on
crossing the one hundred and eightieth meridian of longitude,
just half-way around the world from London, and equidis-
tant, east and west, from the observatory at Greenwich.
Some wicked passengers ascribed our stormy weather to the

missionaries on board, claiming that gales at sea are their invariable attendants. However that may be, there certainly were times when all the passengers (missionaries included) would have agreed with the old Japanese proverb—"A stormy sea-voyage is an inch of hell."

Nothing stands out more clearly in my recollection of the Orient than the bright, long anticipated hour when, after thirteen days of dreary ocean travel, we suddenly beheld, emerging from the waves, that strange, unique, and fascinating land, which promised so much novelty and pleasure,— old Japan. Old, and yet new; for the fair sheet of water which first greeted us was Mississippi Bay, named from the flagship of Commodore Perry, which, with the remainder of his American fleet, dropped anchor here in 1854. The coming of this envoy to the East was not for the purpose of war or invasion, but to request that this important empire, our nearest neighbor westward, lying directly in the path of commerce between Asia and America, should, for the sake of mutual benefit, open its doors (till then resolutely closed to foreigners) and become, to some degree, accessible to the outer world.

COMING TO MEET US.

Impatient to explore this land, we swept the shore with field-glasses, and saw, with much amusement, some natives hastening to launch their boats and row out to us. But were they really coming in just that economical style of dress? They were, and did; but in five minutes we forgot their costumes (or rather their want of them) in admiration of the men themselves. It was, however, not their faces, but their forms, which so attracted us. Never in marble or in bronze have I seen finer specimens of limbs and muscles than those displayed by the compactly built and copper-colored boatmen of Japan. Some of them looked like masterpieces of antiquity, suddenly endowed with life and motion.

Taking the hotel steam-launch, in preference to the native boats, we quickly reached the landing-pier of Yokohama. A slight examination of our trunks was made by officers polite enough to beg our pardon for the trifling delay. There is a duty in Japan on photographic cameras. One of our party was, therefore, called upon to pay the stipulated sum. "I have no Japanese money," he faltered; "I must leave my camera here, and call again."

"Not at all," replied the official courteously; "I will lend

THE CUSTOM HOUSE, YOKOHAMA.

you the money; here it is." I thought my friend, accustomed only to the refinements of the New York Customhouse, would faint away. At last he gathered strength enough to ask: "But what security have you that I will repay you?"

"Ah!" replied the officer, smiling, "you are an American."

AS THE NATIVES TRAVEL.

"Truly," he exclaimed, as we walked away, "the Japanese are the French of Asia."

On leaving the Custom-house I laughed aloud to see awaiting us the almost universal means of locomotion in Japan—the jinrikisha. Shades of our childhood!—what are these? Big-wheeled baby-carriages surely, and yet used altogether by adults. They looked as though a

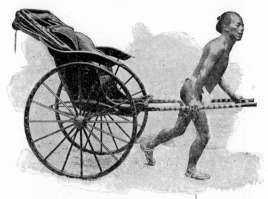

A JINRIKISHA.

heavy man could crush them to earth, or a strong wind might blow them against the wall. When we stepped into ours, we did so cautiously, lest we should suddenly go over backward; and at the sight of some of our more stalwart passengers thus installed, the air was filled with peals of laughter. One portly traveler, weighing at least two hundred pounds, wagged his head feebly at an equally heavy comrade, and shook a "da-da" at him, as if they had both gone back to the state of babyhood. Yet, incredible as it would at first appear, the traveler soon comes to like these little vehicles. Their running-gear, though light, is strong. A breakdown in them is practically unknown. The steeds which draw them harness and unharness themselves, never shy nor kick, and are obedient to the slightest command. Jinrikishas are so cheap that one can hire them all day long and never feel the expense. Ten cents an hour is the usual price, or seventy-five cents for an entire day. One's packages and valises follow in another jinrikisha. The speed at which one travels in them is astonishing.

Even with only one man in the shafts, the usual rate is at least five miles an hour. With one man pushing, and two pulling tandem, you actually seem to fly. On good roads with two men we sometimes made ten miles an hour. And what is most delightful to the traveler, the runners themselves seem to enjoy it thoroughly. Time and again in the country, when they had drawn us twenty or thirty miles with but

A JAPANESE MACKINTOSH.

occasional halts, they actually raced each other on the last half-mile, laughing and capering like boys at play.

In stormy weather these human horses wore blankets that excited both our laughter and amazement. They are a kind of Japanese mackintosh, composed of grass and straw, which, though they are quite effectual in shedding rain and snow, give to the wearer the appearance of a fretful porcupine.

A certain patriotic feeling draws Americans to the jinriki-sha; for this convenient little chaise was the invention of a Yankee missionary. He ought to have made a fortune by it,

PECULIAR TRAVELING.

for in Yokohama alone there are five thousand of these vehicles, and in Japan more than two hundred and fifty thousand; while they are also numerous now in China, India, and Singapore. But the missionary has had the usual fate of inventors, and is said to be, at present, an inmate of an Old Men's Home near Philadelphia.

The Japanese word, jinrikisha, is worth explaining. "jin" means man, "riki" denotes power, and "sha" signifies wheel. A "man-power-carriage" is therefore the correct translation; but the wittiest and most appropriate title is the one given to it by an American tourist,—the "Pull-man-car." Delighted with our first experiences in these little vehicles, we left the Custom-house in Yokohama, and were quickly trundled to the Grand Hotel. This is one of the best hotels in the entire East. It fronts directly on the sea, and one can sit for hours on its long verandas and watch the animated scenes of

"A BIG-WHEELED BABY-CARRIAGE."

street-life in the foreground; or else look off upon the lovely bay, where ships and steamers of all nations lie at anchor, among which glide the native boats, propelled by the bronzed athletes of Japan. My mind goes back with positive delight to some cool morning hours at my window here, but oftener still to moonlit evenings passed upon my balcony. At such a time, the scene recalled a painting in some cyclorama,—so difficult was it to discern where fancy ended and reality began; so smooth appeared the harbor's silvered breast; so motionless the mighty steamers stationed there

WAITING FOR A " FARE."

like sentinels; so still their tapering masts, rising like minarets against the sky; while here and there a red or green light on a steamer's side flashed like a ruby or an emerald. Moreover, as the hours moved on, breaking the solemn stillness of the scene, the ship's bells followed one another through the watches of the night, and stole across the water like a silvery chime.

Yokohama is divided into three sections. The first is the original business settlement, where the hotels are located; the second is the strictly Japanese quarter; the third lies on an eminence called "The Bluff." The summit of this hill is reached, not merely by a winding road, but also by a stair-

A DISTANT VIEW OF FUJI-YAMA.

IN YOKOHAMA BAY.

way commonly known as the "Hundred Steps." Upon this height most of the foreigners reside; here also are the hospitals of different nations, the foreign cemetery, and several consulates. Wishing one day to make a call upon a resident on this hill, and being unable to make our human pony understand his name, we asked the aid of the hotel proprietor. To our astonishment, he said to us: "No name is necessary. I shall merely tell him to take you to gentleman No. 35." A moment's thought explained to us the reason for this custom; for "No. 35 gentleman" or "No. 76 lady" are terms which "'rikisha men" can much more easily understand than foreign names. Yet even this system has its difficulties; for all the houses on the Bluff are numbered, not in the sequence of location, but in the order of their erection. Thus, the first residence constructed

AN OLD-FASHIONED CRAFT.

there is No. 1, but the dwelling next to it, if recently erected, may be called No. 500.

Some of the houses on the Bluff are quite attractive; and life in them must be in many respects delightful. We met

A RESIDENCE ON THE BLUFF.

here two American ladies, who, having taken a furnished house for several months, were actually housekeeping in Japan. They told us that they had never had so pleasant an experience, and that the markets of Yokohama abounded in meat, fish, fruit, and vegetables, all at reasonable prices, while their Japanese servants had been so devoted and respectful that they were spoiled for housekeeping with any others. The summer, they confessed, had been hot, and varied by an occasional earthquake; but on the Bluff the air was pure and cool, and they had at least been exempt from thunder-storms.

Yet Yokohama's climate is not always tropical, or even mild. Winter also can assert itself here, and boats and buildings sometimes wear a robe of snow. Such a wintry temperature makes, of course, little difference in the comfort of foreigners; but, to the Japanese themselves, one might suppose the winter months would be a season of protracted misery, since the vast majority of the natives have no fire in their houses save that in a charcoal brazier; the partitions in their dwellings are mere paper screens; and they themselves rarely wear woolen garments, much less flannel ones. Yet the people are hardy. Jinrikisha men, we were told, will run about the snow-covered streets with only cotton sandals on their feet.

"How can your people live thus thinly clad, and with so little fire?" we asked our guide.

"Oh, they become used to it," he answered. "You never cover up your face in winter. It is accustomed to the cold. So we subject our bodies to the same endurance."

One day, in strolling through a street in Yokohama, we came upon two little Japanese women doing laundry work and spreading garments out to dry upon a smooth, flat board. Following the pleasant custom of the country, they laughingly called out to us, "Ohaio—Ohaio,"—the Japanese expression for "Good Morning!" One of our party, a judge from Covington, Kentucky, did not understand the meaning of that word. Accordingly, when one of these Japanese maidens smiled sweetly in his face, and said, with a slightly rising inflection, "Ohaio!" he faltered, and replied, "Well, not exactly; I come from Covington, just across the river!"

YOKOHAMA IN WINTER.

The foreign cemetery of Yokohama is beautifully situated on the Bluff, above the tumult of the town. It is well kept, and many of its monuments are elaborate. Numerous

ON THE WAY TO KAMAKURA.

epitaphs in English, French, German, and Italian attest the cosmopolitan character of the place. As we were walking there one Sunday afternoon, we met a lady deeply veiled, leaning upon her husband's arm, and giving way to uncontrollable grief. When they were gone we ventured to approach the grave which they had left. The tombstone bore a recent date, and on it were four lines that deeply moved us by their sad simplicity; for, stooping down to a low headstone wreathed in flowers, we read these words:

"A little grave, but oh, have care,
For world-wide hopes are lying there;
How much of light, how much of joy
Are buried with a darling boy!"

The day after our arrival in Yokohama, we drove out into the surrounding country.

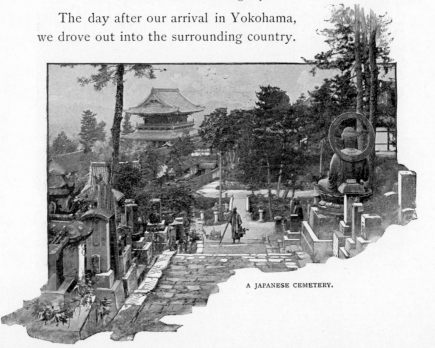

A JAPANESE CEMETERY.

PATH TO THE SHOGUN'S GRAVE.

THE FOREIGN CEMETERY, YOKOHAMA.

It was histori-
cally very inter-
esting.   Upon
the plain where
we saw laborers
harvesting their
c r o p s ,   o n c e
stood the an-
cient capital of
the empire,—
Kamakura.   It
was then the
residence of a
million people,
and was, no doubt, a scene of splendor, war, and intrigue;
yet of the men and deeds which moved it centuries ago
we know comparatively nothing.   We sometimes think our-

selves familiar
with the history
of our race; and
so we are, along
the lines of
Egypt, Rome,
and mediæval
Europe.   But
when the trav-
eler visits China,
India, and Japan,
he realizes the
fact that he has
come to the other
side of the globe,
—to lands whose
histories are

DOING LAUNDRY WORK.

more remote than those of even Greece and Rome, and yet
utterly distinct from all the streams of civilization which
have flowed toward him. He begins to feel as men might
who, having always thought the Rhine to be the only river
of any magnitude on earth, should suddenly find themselves
beside the Nile, whose mighty volume has been rolling
onward for unnumbered ages, and over whose distant origin
there hangs the halo of mystery.

One thing, however, still remains at Kamakura to tell us
of its unrecorded past. It is the world-renowned statue of
Buddha,—one of the largest works in bronze that man has
ever made. Upon a huge stone pedestal, in the form of a
lotus-flower, 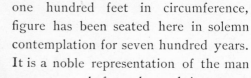 one hundred feet in circumference,
this monstrous figure has been seated here in solemn
contemplation for seven hundred years.
It is a noble representation of the man

before whose shrines more
knees are bent in prayer
to-day than before those
of any other founder
of religion whom this
earth has known.
Close by, beneath the
trees, are pedestals of
enormous columns,
the relics of a splen-
did temple which once
formed the canopy of the
statue, but which was
swept away by a huge
tidal wave, four hundred
years ago. The statue
itself, however, was too
immense and weighty to

A BUDDHIST
PAGODA.

be thus destroyed; hence, as it sits here now in solitary
grandeur on a plain, beneath which sleeps a vanished world,
the only columns that surround
it are majestic trees, the only
roof that shelters
it is the arch of
the immeasurable
sky, and the only
tapers on its ruined
altar are the un-
changing stars.

It is easy to
enumerate statis-
tics here; to
call to mind
the fact that
this statue is
fifty feet in
height; that
underneath its
drooping lids
are eyes of
purest gold;

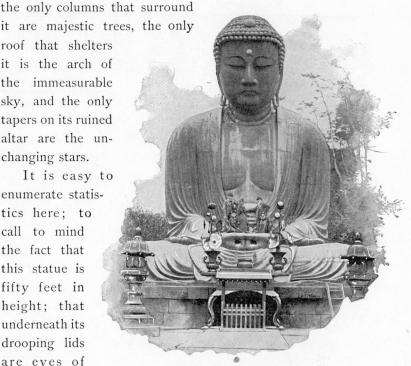

THE BRONZE BUDDHA AT KAMAKURA.

that the face alone is eighteen feet in length; that the circumference of the thumb is three feet; and, finally, that within
this statue is a chapel for a hundred worshipers. But these
are not the things which most impress one here. We can
find other statues for statistics. This has something better.
It is the indescribable, passionless expression of the face, that
grows upon the traveler as he studies it, and haunts his memory forever more—a look which in some way suggests the
Sphinx, in its superiority to present evils, its dreamful contemplation of the infinite, its calm appeal from time to all
eternity.

ENOSHIMA.

Leaving the great Buddha to his meditations, we continued our homeward journey by the sea,—that ocean which, although tranquil now, has more than once sent tidal waves upon this shore to wreck the temples and the homes of Kamakura, and in their swift retreat to leave a hideous trail of death and devastation. A little distance from the land, we saw the pretty island of Enoshima. It is a sacred island, said to have sprung, like Venus, from the ocean in a single night. It is regarded, therefore, as a gift from God. It may be that the legend has some truth in it, for almost every portion of Japan is of volcanic origin; and mountains have arisen, lakes have been produced, and landscapes wholly changed by earthquake shocks, even within historical times.

Desiring to see some features of this

JACOB'S LADDER, ENOSHIMA.

A FOREST MONARCH.

INTERIOR OF THE CAVERN TEMPLE.

island, we crossed the narrow channel, and climbed to one of its numerous points of observation. It is a fascinating place. Delightful paths wind up the wooded hills, marked here and there by little stations, where one halts for tea. Beyond these are long flights of steps, on which, that afternoon, Japanese girls, in gaily-colored robes, were passing up and down, like angels upon Jacob's ladder. Some were at work, while others were at play; others, again, were returning from a place of prayer. They looked as curiously at us as we at them. We seemed to them, no doubt, like beings from another world; probably not a better one, for, when we had walked on, we heard them

THE SACRED CAVE.

merrily discussing us with peals of child-like laughter. One part of Enoshima is deemed especially sacred. It is a natural cavern, somewhat resembling the Blue Grotto on

A RUSTIC BUDDHA.

the Island of Capri. In stormy weather it is inaccessible, for furious waves then thunder for admission here, and fill the entrance with a mass of foam. But on a pleasant day, like that which we enjoyed, it is not very difficult, on

coming down the hill, to cross a wooden bridge and a few
slippery rocks, and finally pass beneath a frowning arch to
the interior.

It is a singular opening,—a crack in the volcanic cliff,
three hundred feet in length and thirty in height. From its
obscure recesses, we gained a charming telescopic vista of
the broad Pacific. To our astonishment, we found within
this cave an altar to the goddess of Good Fortune, a deity
that from remotest ages has been worshiped here. It is a wonderful situation for an altar, this rock-hewn temple built by
Nature's architect. A kind of mystery surrounds it, for mor-
tals cannot al-
ways worship
here. When
the divinity al-
lows them to
approach, this
inlet of the
ocean lies in ab-
solute tranquil-
lity, extending
inward to the
shrine, like a

A JAPANESE RAILWAY.

long path of malachite. But there are times when she excludes
all worshipers, bars the majestic portal with a watery wall, and
hears, instead of humanity's feeble voice, the awe-inspiring
anthem of the sea.

One beautiful October morning, leaving the Grand Hotel,
we drove to the railway station to take a train for the Japanese capital, Tokio, eighteen miles distant. It seemed a
wonderful transition to whirl through Yokohama streets in
baby-carriages drawn by half-naked natives, and in a moment
more to find ourselves in railroad cars, better arranged in some
respects than most trains that run in Europe. Such sudden

contrasts between the past and present are now found only in Japan. Twenty-five years ago there were no railways here, and hardly a jinrikisha. To-day, throughout this sea-girt empire is spread a network of two thousand miles of well-built paths of steel, which have stone ballast, massive bridges, fine rolling-stock, and well-appointed stations. And yet one travels first-class in Japan almost as cheaply as third-class in Europe. Nor is traveling in the Mikado's realm confined to foreigners. Never in any portion of the world have I seen trains so uniformly thronged as here, and ninety out of every hundred of the passengers were Japanese.

Tokio is the same old Yeddo that figured in our schoolbooks—no matter how many years ago. The first thing to impress me in the place was its enormous size. It is, in truth, a city of magnificent distances,

THE IMPERIAL HOTEL, TOKIO.

for its area surpasses that of London. Together with its suburbs, it has a population of one million eight hundred thousand. Save for its vast extent, however, the Japanese

A TORII.

capital is not imposing. Seen from an elevation Tokio displays an almost limitless expanse of wooden roofs, whose trifling inequalities recall the undulating surface of a cold, gray sea. From this there rises, here and there, a solitary tower or pagoda, like a lighthouse from the waves.

LOOKING DOWN UPON TOKIO.

Four hundred years ago Tokio was a fishing hamlet. Not until 1603 did it become the military capital; and since that time it has been so frequently burned down and rebuilt, that it may be compared to the human body, the particles of which are said at certain intervals to be entirely renewed. In fact, statistics prove that, on an average, the city every thirty years has risen anew from its ashes. In 1895, at a single fire, four thousand houses were destroyed.

It is no easy task to explore thoroughly the Japanese labyrinth called Tokio, but one great central object forms, at least, a starting point,—the imperial palace. Around it, like a warrior's belt, is drawn a moat so broad and deep that it might easily be deemed a river. The vast extent of this enclosure, its highly finished wall of stone, the silent, waveless stretch of water which surrounds it,—all these add mystery to one whose residence is so secluded from the eyes of men. Yet it is only recently that the Mikado has lived here. Thirty years ago the residence of Japanese sovereigns was a retired palace in the ancient city of Kioto. It may well be called "retired," for previous to the revolution of 1869 (which may be called the new birth of Japan) the Japanese for centuries had never seen the face of the Mikado. In giving audiences, even to his priests and nobles, he sat invisible behind a screen. When he walked out within his garden, carpets were spread before him to keep his sacred feet from contact with the earth. If he drove out, it was in a covered carriage, closed by screens,

BRIDGE TO THE EMPEROR'S PALACE, TOKIO.

and as he passed along his subjects knelt in the attitude of prayer. Thus, century after century, these sovereigns lived, —each one in turn a monarch yet a captive, a god and yet a slave.

Meanwhile, in one of the stately castles of Japan there lived the Mikado's representative, or viceroy; for, of course, the Japanese emperors did not govern. How could they? They were imprisoned by their own divinity. A mediator between the monarch and his subjects had to be appointed, to act as overseer of the realm. Previous to 1869 therefore —for nearly seven hundred years—two rulers had existed in

Japan. One was the theoretical sovereign, to whom all gave allegiance, but who accomplished nothing,— the Mikado; the

SHOGUN'S PALACE, OSAKA.

other was the practical executive,— the military regent, called the Shogun.

In the small town of Shizuoka we saw the modest house where was still residing, like a country gentleman, the last of the once powerful Shoguns of Japan; for a change has taken place in the Mikado's empire. The Shoguns, who for centuries had been the actual sovereigns of the realm, and one of whom was in full power when the American fleet arrived in Yokohama, have now completely disappeared. Less than thirty years

THE MOAT AROUND THE PALACE, TOKIO.

ago, from the secret precincts of his palace in Kioto, the lawful ruler, the present Mikado, was brought to light, like one who had been immured within a dungeon. In 1872, for the first time in a thousand years, a Japanese emperor freely appeared before his subjects. He was at that time a young man, twenty-two

HOME OF THE RETIRED SHOGUN, SHIZUOKA.

years of age, and was actually traveling by rail from Yokohama to Tokio, thenceforth to make that city his abode and capital. On that occasion, we are told, the loyalty and enthusiasm of his subjects knew no bounds. As the train moved off with the young emperor, restored to his ancestral power, there rang out on the air a melody which thrilled all hearts. It was the national anthem of Japan, the strains of which were first heard when savage tribes were hunting by the

WHERE SOME OF THE SHOGUNS ARE BURIED.

NEAR A HERO'S GRAVE.

Thames and Rome was mistress of the world.

One might suppose that such a sudden rise in power, combined with the amazing changes in his empire, would

SHOGUN'S RESIDENCE, NAGOYA.

have been ruinous to this young sovereign, for at the time of the restoration he was but sixteen years old. But he was evidently the man for the occasion, and has since proved himself an assiduous student and enlightened ruler. This man,

ENTRANCE TO THE SHOGUNS' TEMPLE, TOKIO.

who, as a youth, knew almost nothing of the existence of such foreign lands, now reads the literatures of England, France,

OLD FEUDAL RESIDENCE, TOKIO.

and Germany. Moreover, this hundred and twenty-first Mikado of his line—the representative of the oldest dynasty on earth, whose founder reigned here five hundred years before the death of Julius Cæsar,— has not only adopted European dress and customs, but has favored the introduction of all the great inventions of the present age. Nevertheless, he had the wisdom to restrain his subjects in their first eagerness to adopt everything European, when they were even ready to destroy, as worthless, some of their ancient castles, shrines, and statues. And now that a reaction has set in, and the Japanese are once

A MODERN CASTLE.

more proud to cherish the memorials of their ancestors, they are sincerely grateful to their emperor, because at the great national crisis he showed sufficient tact and independence to steer between the rocks of servile imitation on the one side and dull conservatism on the other, and, while the ship of state was trembling in the rapids of that flood of progress, he maintained a firm hand on the helm.

The houses of the old Japanese nobles in Tokio recall many other striking contrasts between the past and the present. Until recently, for nearly a thousand years, Japan had many feudal lords, called Daimios. Most of them lived in Tokio for at least six months of every year, under the Shogun's watchful eye. But the great revolution of 1869 completely swept away the feudalism of centuries, and one by one, at the command of the Mikado, the Daimios gave up their swords, dismissed their armed retainers, renounced, to some extent, their vast estates and revenues, and, as a rule, retired to private life.

A LADY OF TOKIO.

Yet one must not suppose that the Japan of the present day has no nobility. Some years ago there was a grand revision of all ranks and titles. The old, distinguished families still form the nucleus of the aristocracy; but to their ranks have been added many men conspicuous for their talents, or for their loyalty to the new *régime*. We had the pleasure of meeting one who lives in close relations with the emperor. We found him a refined and courteous gentleman, dressed in a faultless suit of broadcloth, and speaking

AN OLD-TIME SWORDSMAN.

French and English fluently. As we conversed with him, however, our thoughts would stray from his appearance to that which his own father, doubtless, had presented, when Commodore Perry moored his fleet in Mississippi Bay. For his father had been one of those warriors of old Japan, called Samurai. A certain number of these men adhered to every Daimio, lived at his castle, fought his battles, and, not content with one sword, always carried two, as distinctive symbols of their rank. Yet now the old-time swordsman, if alive, has no doubt ceased to shave his head, has laid aside his singular costume, and has even put his swords away as relics of his youthful days,

AN OLD-FASHIONED DUEL, AND UMPIRE.

CENTENARIAN TREES.

since no civilian is at present allowed to wear them. It is said that this class of Japanese suffered most from the revolution, for they suddenly found their occupation completely gone. Untrained for work and ill-adapted to the sudden change, their situation was at first deplorable. Hence it is little short of marvelous that such a radical transformation could have been effected in Japan without frequent insurrections. The sight of this great nation turning from feudalism to a constitutional

THE PRINCIPAL THEATRE IN TOKIO.

monarchy, at the cost of rank, fame, wealth, and even livelihood, for tens of thousands of its foremost citizens, gives proof of a wide-spread, unselfish patriotism, perhaps unequaled in the world's history.

Not less remarkable is the recent progress of education in this "Land of the Rising Sun." The educational systems of all other nations have ripened slowly, and rest on centuries of experience. But twenty-five years ago, Japan had practically nothing of the kind. Accordingly, her brightest and most promising youths went forth to gather knowledge in the western world. She was eclectic in her method. Some were sent to England, some to Germany, others to France, and many to America. Accomplished foreign teachers also were induced to come and give instruction in Japanese schools; and how astonishing has been the result! In Tokio the buildings of the Imperial University cover fifteen acres of ground, and in-

A JAPANESE ACTOR.

clude admirable class-rooms, dormitories, laboratories, a hospital, and residences for the faculty. Here, in one department, are taught mathematics, astronomy, chemistry and geology; in another, civil and electrical engineering, naval architecture and metallurgy; in another, philosophy and the modern European languages; in still another, Japanese and Chinese history and literature. The University has also a Law School and a College of Medicine and Pharmacy, in each of which a four years' course is required. There are in all one hundred and twenty-three professors in the institution, fifteen of whom are foreigners, while more than fifty lecturers are also in the employ of the directors. Nor is this

A SACRED GATE.

all, for in addition to this splendid University, there are in Tokio private colleges, commercial schools, military and naval academies, and a school of fine arts, besides an educational institution for the dumb and the blind; and not the least noteworthy is a common school system whereby the poorest child in Japan may obtain at least a rudimentary education.

IN WINTER COSTUME.

Let no one think, however, that all these changes, surprising though they are, have wholly done away with "old" Japan. The contrary is proved by countless characteristic sights, even in modernized Tokio. In their houses, theatres, shops, and festivals, and in their modes of bathing, eating, drinking, sleeping, and working, the vast majority of Japanese are to-day what they were centuries ago.

On our first day in Tokio, as we descended from the hill where we had gained a comprehensive view of the great city,

A DAIMIO'S HOME, TOKIO.

we paused to note, at the foot of a long stone staircase, a singular gateway built of granite. The tourist may well observe such structures closely, for one of the most common architectural features of Japan is this peculiar style of portal, called a *torii*. In granite, wood, or bronze, such gateways usually mark the approach to a temple, shrine, or sacred statue. Nothing could be more simple. Two upright shafts are met and crossed by horizontal bars, the higher ones curving slightly upward at the ends. This is in one sense all, and the beholder

A TORII OR SACRED GATE.

at first sees little in them to admire; but, after a time, the foreigner in Japan expects them as essential features of every landscape, and welcomes them, like some sweet refrain, which, first heard in the overture, repeats itself in various disguises through the music of an opera.

There are two theories in regard to the origin of these sacred portals. The first maintains that they were intended originally for perches, upon which birds (which are occasionally liberated even now at Japanese temples) might pause before they took their heavenward flight to bear aloft the

A RUSTIC TORII.

prayers of those who gave them freedom. The second theory affirms that these straight columns, with their curving cross-pieces, are derivative forms of the Chinese letter, or ideograph, which signifies Heaven. The latter explanation appears to be the more probable one; at all events, whatever may have been their origin, the architectural design of these peculiar structures is of immense antiquity. Such gateways, tradition hints, were extant twenty centuries ago; and it is worthy of remark that, despite the marvelous changes that have recently transformed Japan, no hand has ever been raised to mutilate these memorials of the past, or even to change a line of that mysterious hieroglyph which they so sharply outline against the sky.

A GROUP OF TORII.

In the immediate vicinity of these sacred arches, one usually sees a multitude of monuments, from five to seven feet in height. Sometimes these line, for a considerable distance, the avenues of approach to tombs and temples, and are compactly ranged in serried ranks, like soldiers at a dress parade, or people waiting for some grand procession. They are called lanterns, from the fact that, on special festivals, a

JAPANESE LANTERNS.

lamp is placed in each of them, in honor of the hallowed dead. But the chief part they play is ornamental. Most of them are of stone; but some consist of beautifully decorated bronze,—real masterpieces of that art in which the Japanese excel. To many are attached bronze bells and circular medallions, bearing the crests of the imperial family or those of the military chieftains of Japan. With few exceptions, the finest ones have been presented by Japanese nobles, as

APPROACH TO THE TEMPLES, NIKKO.

proofs of their devotion to the shrine itself, or their esteem for those who are buried there.

One of the principal pleasure-resorts of Tokio is Ueno

IN SERRIED RANKS.

Park. It is especially attractive in the month of April, when all its cherry-trees are radiant with blossoms. These

A BRONZE LANTERN.

lovely flowers are usually pink in color, and grow in clusters several inches wide. Poets have sung their praises here for centuries. They are to Japan what roses are to western nations. Their blooming-time is one of the national festivals. Some avenues in the Mikado's capital are lined with these resplendent trees, and are famous throughout

BLOSSOM-LADEN BANKS.

the country for their wealth of coloring. There is a little stream in Tokio which, every year, about the middle of April, flows for two miles between blossom-laden banks. Crowds gather then from miles around, to gaze upon its beauty. The newspapers announce each day the progress of the coloring, and maps of the city are sold, on which are indicated in pink the groves of cherry-trees. Old Mother Earth grows young again, and every heart, however sad, becomes rejuvenated too, at the sight of thousands of these huge bouquets, lifting their clouds of pale

A JAPANESE TEMPLE.

pink blossoms toward the light blue sky. Hundreds of pleasure-boats also then float along the stream, which mirrors the gorgeous spectacle above. A Japanese poet says: "I wish to cross the river, but fear to cut the brocade upon its surface." Meanwhile, along the banks are thousands of other admirers, on foot or in jinrikishas; and not infrequently a mischievous breeze plucks handfuls of the dainty petals and scatters them upon the up-turned faces, like flakes of tinted snow.

As we might expect from such a refined and artistic race, the Japanese are enthusiastic in their love of flowers. One of their favorite deities is called "The Goddess who causes the blossoms to open." With them, to make up parties for a floral exhibition is just as fashionable as for us to arrange box-parties for the theatre. Even in winter they will not allow themselves to be deprived of some enjoyment of this sort. Hence they call snow-crystals a kind of flower, and expeditions to see snow-displays form one of the regular amusements of the season.

A TEA-HOUSE ORNAMENTED WITH WISTARIA.

The land of the Mikado is with reason often called the Land of Flowers, for each month of the year has its special blossoms which the Japanese admire, and which together

form an unbroken garland for the brow of Time. Particularly
beautiful is the Japanese wistaria, which blooms in May,

soon after the departure of
the cherry-blossoms. This
lovely vine is trained on
trellises, and covers bridges,
canopies, and arbors with
magnificent purple clusters,
two, and even three feet
long. Japanese tea-houses
find it extremely profitable
to decorate their gardens
thus, as thousands are attracted thither, who, as a

A DWARF MAPLE.

matter of course, drink tea upon the premises. It is precisely of such exhibitions that this peculiar nation is most
fond. With one or two exceptions, they do not seem to
care for cultivated flowers, preferring flowering trees and
vines, like the wistaria, plum, and cherry. In all the gardens
that we visited in Japan, we never saw a flower-bed. In
fact, Japanese gardens differ from our own as completely as a
jinrikisha differs from a tally-ho coach. They are all essential-
ly alike,   whether
they   cover

THE GREAT TREE NEAR LAKE BIWA.

FOREST SOLITUDE.

several acres or only a tiny court behind the house. If possible, an artificial lake is formed; large, if the space permits;
if not, a little tank of water containing half-a-dozen goldfish
must suffice. Rocks are heaped up to take the place of cliffs.
A path of pebbles represents a river-bed. A tiny beach of
smooth, white sand is made along the shore. Islands are also
manufactured, with fantastic bridges; and here and there
among the trees we see a quaint display of garden lanterns, miniature
pagodas, foun-
tains, grottoes,
and occasional
statues. But of
smooth lawns
and ornamental
flowers, like our
own, we find in
Japanese gar-
dens not a trace.
What seems to
take their place
in the affections
of the Japanese
is the cultivation

JAPANESE LANDSCAPE GARDENING.

of dwarf trees. These are among the marvels of Japan. At
first, we could hardly believe our eyes, when we saw maples,
pines, and oaks, from sixty to one hundred years old, possessing crooked limbs and gnarled and twisted trunks, though
they were scarcely more than two feet high, and had their
roots confined within the limits of a flower-pot! Just what
the secret is of limiting the growth of these old monarchs of
the forest, while yet preserving their vitality, we did not
learn. It is, however, an art of which the Japanese are pas-
sionately fond, and which an experience of centuries has

brought to perfection.   These hardy dwarfs are often looked
upon as precious heirlooms, and are carefully watched and
tended by the family from generation to generation.   What
a strange notion this,—of dwarfing landscapes to the limit
of a courtyard, and stunting noble trees till they appear like
a forest looked at through the large end of a telescope!
Sometimes, however, the taste of the
Japanese in arboriculture goes to

A TREE TRIMMED TO
REPRESENT A SHIP.

the other extreme, and large trees are chosen as objects
of regard.   These are often trained and trimmed, till they
resemble mammoth fans, pagodas, or stately boats with curving prows and lofty masts adorned with tiny sails.   Although ingenious, this seemed to us like trifling with nature,—a parody of the sublime,—a burlesque of the beautiful.
    The glory of the month of August in Japan is the sacred
lotus-flower, with whose broad leaves the moats in Tokio are
filled.   Growing from muddy, stagnant water, yet holding

up to heaven its flowers always fresh and pure, the lotus is regarded as the symbol of the religious life,—aspiring from

unfavorable conditions to a state of purity. The Buddhist writings say: "Though thou be born in a hovel, if thou hast virtue, thou art like the lotus growing from the slime." Accordingly the

A LOTUS BED.

lotus is, *par excellence*, the flower of the Buddhist faith, associated with the mysteries of death and immortality. Bronze vases, filled with lotus-flowers made of metal, stand on all Buddhist altars, and statues of Buddha have usually, as an appropriate pedestal, a smooth lotus-leaf in stone or bronze. Early November brings still another source of pleasure to the

STATUES OF BUDDHA WITH LOTUS PEDESTALS.

THE NATIONAL FLOWER.

Japanese in the chrysanthe-mum. Opin-ions differ as to whether this, or the cherry-blossom, should be regarded as the Japanese national flower. To us it seemed that the chrys-anthemum should have that proud dis-tinction; for it is used as the crest of the imperial family; and the Mikado's birthday, the third of November, is usually made the opening day for all chrysanthemum exhibitions. In cultivating this flower, the Japanese have shown extraor-dinary skill. Some of their bushes are said to bear as many as four hundred perfect flowers at one time. Five or six vari-eties sometimes grow upon a single plant, and there are claimed to be, in all, two hun-dred and sixty-

AUTUMNAL FOLIAGE.

THE MODERNIZING RAILWAY.

nine in the Mikado's empire. Moreover, since it blossoms
longer than most other flowers, it is associated with the idea
of longevity. One Japanese river, into whose limpid waters
great showers of chrysanthemum petals fall, is thought to
insure to a good old age the lives of those who drink from its
invigorating flood.

But perhaps the most gorgeous of the natural displays,
which in Japan adorn with a continuous brilliancy the path
of the revolving
year, is its au-
tumnal foliage.
Then, as the
Japanese poets
say, the maple-
trees put on
their damask
robes. This
also is thought
to be a floral
exhibition, for
bright-colored
leaves are looked
upon by the
Japanese as

A WRESTLING MATCH.

flowers. The subjects of the Mikado have, like ourselves,
that most delicious season of the year when the warm breath
of summer still retards the frost. We call it Indian Summer:
their name for it is Little Spring. It is a pretty—almost a
pathetic—thought, to connect thus the deep, strong, passion-
ate hues that mark the year's maturity with the faint blushes
of the cherry-blossoms, which betoken youth. The year has
lived through much since that pink blush adorned its cheeks.
The autumnal colors may be richer and more effective, but
that first bloom of hope and innocence will never come again.

During our stay in Tokio, we one day visited a wrestling match. The scene of its occurrence, though in the heart of the city, resembled the enclosure of a country circus. On pushing through the crowd, we saw, in the centre, an elevated platform covered with sand. Above this was a highly decorated canopy, supported by tall bamboo poles, and gathered round it was the expectant populace. The second story of the structure consisted of a gallery made of bamboo rods, which, tied together, formed a floor resembling an enormous gridiron. This gallery was divided into little areas, which served as private boxes for the entertainment.

A WRESTLER.

We climbed up into one of these by means of a ladder, and tea and cakes were subsequently brought to us; but we could not have eaten a mouthful, unless fed by our attendant, for we were fully occupied in clinging to the bamboo poles, like canary birds to their perches. There presently appeared upon the stage a human monster, who seemed to have a gorgeous lambrequin tied about his waist. This giant was a great surprise to us. The Japanese are usually small; their women seem like girls; their children look like dolls; their dwellings have the appearance of magnified bird-cages; their vehicle of transportation is a baby-carriage. Their wrestlers, however, are enormous. Such mountainous displays of fat and muscle we had never seen. One after

another, fifty such giants stood fronting us for a moment
with uplifted arms, while an official read their names to the
admiring spectators. Twenty-five wrestlers were then chosen
to contend on one side and as many on the other. The prize
was to be given to whichever side should win the greatest
number of single combats.

A moment later, the "lambrequins" were laid aside. A
couple of huge wrestlers squatted on the sand, like mammoth bull-frogs ready for a jump. They had already rubbed
their hands in the sand to make them gritty and tenacious.
Beside them stood the umpire, holding in his hand a fan.
With this he gave his signal to the wrestlers, much as a
musical director leads his orchestra. His word is law, and he
decides whether the start is properly made and whether the

rules have been
observed. A
few false springs
were made at
first, and the
great crowd be-
came impatient.
At last, how-
ever, the wrest-
lers fairly caught
each other, and
began the strug-
gle. For sev-
eral minutes
they tugged and
strained, until it

LIKE MAMMOTH BULL-FROGS.

seemed that neither could possibly gain the advantage.
Meantime the Japanese grew more and more excited, for
all these wrestlers are well known, and have their patrons and
admirers. One whom we saw is famous for having thrown

AN ACROBAT.

three rivals in succession. This is, of course, a proof of great endurance; for by the time the third encounter comes, the victor must necessarily be much exhausted. In the first match, however, the wrestlers whom we watched had no easy task; but, presently, one of them saw his opportunity, and caught his enemy under the left leg. The other instantly reached over his shoulder and clutched his opponent's belt. For a few seconds neither moved. Then, with a fearful lurch, the giant who had gained the advantage lifted his rival off the ground, and swung him headlong over his shoulder clear off the platform to the sand below. We felt our bamboo perch in the gallery shake when the body struck. The conqueror was, of course, hailed with shouts of triumph, and in five minutes all was ready for another contest.

"THEY TUGGED AND STRAINED."

At the conclusion of the spectacle, as we were making our exit through the crowd, we stopped to watch some Japanese acrobats, one of whom danced upon a swinging rope with more agility and skill than we had ever seen. "By the way," said a friend at my side, "do you know that once in the history of this country the Japanese throne itself was wrestled for? It happened just a thousand years ago. The Mikado died and left two sons, each of whom claimed to be

VILLAGE OF NIKKO.

the rightful heir. Instead of plunging the nation into civil war, they submitted their rival claims to a couple of famous wrestlers, each agreeing to abide by the result! Who shall say that there are not worse methods than this old Japanese mode of arbitration?"

One of the most renowned and sacred places of resort, alike for pilgrims and for tourists in Japan, is Nikko. "Nikko!" How little that brief name suggests to those whose feet have never trod its hallowed paths; but, oh, how much to those whose recollections of it are a joy forever! The

THE SACRED BRIDGE, NIKKO.

mere approach to it is astonishing. It is a sacred road, over twenty miles in length, and lined for the most part on both sides with the grand cedars of Japan. These trees, called cryptomerias, frequently attain a height of two hundred feet,

TIER UPON TIER AND
TERRACE UPON TERRACE.

CHARACTERISTIC ARCHITECTURE.

and are probably unsurpassed in size save by the giants of
our own Yosemite.

It was late in the afternoon when we reached the terminus
of this avenue. Before us rose a densely wooded mountain,
around which swept a wild, impetuous stream. Spanning
this foaming torrent is the sacred bridge of Nikko, whose
floor and sides are covered with beautiful red lacquer, as

THE ROAD TO NIKKO.

smooth to the touch as polished mahogany, and which is ornamented here and there with tips of brass. In ancient times,
none but the Shoguns ever stepped upon this bridge; none
but the emperor may do so now. When General Grant,
however, was traveling in Japan, the Mikado paid him the
unusual compliment of ordering this bridge to be thrown open
for his passage. But, from a delicate appreciation of the
people's feelings, the General modestly declined the honor,
and took the regular, frequented path.

Leaving behind us this ornate but untrodden bridge, we began to ascend the hill itself. From time to time we halted, astonished and bewildered. Imagine a mountain, covered with thousands of the most magnificent cedar-trees that the

THE PILGRIMS' FOUNTAIN, NIKKO.

Creator ever caused to grow; then realize that upon this mountain and among these trees there is what may be called a sacred citadel, rising tier above tier, and terrace upon terrace, each covering several acres. Toward each plateau ascends a flight of broad stone steps. In front of each is placed the characteristic gateway of Japan,—the sharp-cut, mysterious *torii*, hewn out of massive stone or made of polished bronze. In one place there is a beautifully decorated fountain, at which all pilgrims wash their hands and mouths before approaching more closely to the temples of their gods.

Ascending one of the staircases of stone, we stood in an extensive area, where structures met our gaze so unlike all that we had elsewhere seen that we were fain to believe our senses were deceiving us, and that it was all an illusion,—a cunning trick for stage effect, which, when the play was over, would completely vanish. Along the terraces, like jewels darkened by the forest gloom, were belfries which appeared encased with precious stones; fountains adorned with ornaments of gilded bronze; picturesque temples bright with every color of the rainbow; lacquered pagodas, rivaling the trees in height; and huge bronze bells, whose solemn tones, in rythmic waves of sound, roll on in grand reverberations

ON ONE OF THE TERRACES.

through these sacred avenues. But how powerless is language to portray a place like this! Words impotently creep before the grand impressiveness of Nikko, as insects crawl beneath its cryptomerias.

A GATEWAY AT NIKKO.

As we advanced still farther through these wonderful enclosures, it seemed like walking through a village whose buildings still remained in symmetry and beauty, yet whose inhabitants had   disappeared. The si-   lence of

A QUIET CORNER.

PRIESTLY VESTMENTS.

these courts was most impressive. Apparently, they have no guardians. Only the moss-grown lanterns stand about each shrine, like sentinels transformed to stone. Astonished and perplexed, we

A PROCESSION AT NIKKO.

asked the meaning of these structures, and learned that some are treasure-houses, where are preserved the personal relics of the Shoguns and many of the gorgeous robes,

AMONG THE SHRINES.

embroidered banners, and superb insignia which still, on
festal days, are borne in solemn state along these paths
beneath a boundless canopy of shade, just as they have been

ENTRANCE TO TEMPLE, NIKKO.

borne for centuries.   For the old trees of Nikko have looked
down for nearly a thousand years on lines of richly decorated
priests and pilgrims moving in solemn pageantry along these
shadowy pathways consecrated to the gods.   The individuals
may come and go, but the processions never fail—much as the
bright-tinted leaves fall here in autumn, to return no more,
while the old trees live on.

At last we stood before one of the many sacred gates which lead to Nikko's shrines or sepulchres. Each displays against the foliage beyond a mass of variegated color. In every case the roof curves slightly upward at the base, and has a covering of copper, marked with ornaments in brass. To the right and left of all such passageways are massive wooden columns, lacquered red, and in the alcoves thus constructed at this gate we saw, to our amazement, two grotesque statues of colossal size. They seemed a startling union of Hercules and Mephistopheles. Yet these repulsive figures represent gods, whose special duty is to scare demons from the temple gates. We have no certain information about the nervous temperament of demons, but one could well believe that these unearthly shapes, with blood-red bodies, gaping mouths, and bulging eyes, would throw most children

A TARGET FOR MASTICATED PRAYERS.

into convulsions. Upon their forms and faces are visible small marks resembling scars. These are in reality dried paper-balls, which worshipers have first chewed into a pulp,

and then hurled at the statues, though not by any means in
contempt.   The pilgrim, in the first place, writes his petition
on a slip of paper; this he rolls into a wad, which he de-
posits in his mouth; and, finally, when it is softened by
saliva, he throws it at the god.   If it adheres to the idol's

face, the omen
is propitious.
If it sticks to
any part of the
body, there is
still some hope;
but if it falls off
on the ground,
a favorable an-
swer is impossi-
ble.   This cus-
tom is pecul-
iar to Japan.
One sees, of
course, num-
berless strange
rites connected
with religion in
traveling about
the world, but
Japan is the

A GUARDIAN OF THE GATE.

only land I have ever visited where deities serve as targets
for masticated prayers!

When, turning from these sculptured monsters, one looks
with admiration on the exquisitely carved and beautifully
furnished temples of this sacred citadel, one naturally
exclaims: "How is it possible that the same race, which has
produced such beautiful, artistic works as these, should also
have created, and should still retain, such hideous, uncouth

statues as we
have just be-
held?'' But
one asks many
such questions
in traveling
through Japan.
No race on
earth is so as-
tonishingly con-
tradictory and
so full of puz-
zling surprises
as the Japanese.
'' The longer I
live here,'' a

THE BRONZE PORTAL.

resident of Tokio once said to me, '' the less I understand
these people. A superficial knowledge of them is easily acquired; but there is always at the last a mental gulf between
the Orient and the Occident, across which I perceive that
their past is not our past, and that their ideas on art, religion,

THE PATH TO THE SHOGUN'S GRAVE.

government, the finite and the infinite, are radically different from our own.''

Leaving at length the shrines of Nikko, we climbed still farther up the sa- cred mountain, by one of its great staircases of stone. It led us to a place of which the temples are but antecham- bers and accesso- ries. For this mag- nificent forest is a vast sepul- chral grove, in which are buried some of the great- est statesmen of Japan.

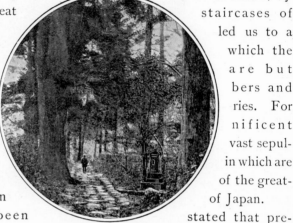

NATURE'S CATHEDRAL.

It has been stated that pre- vious to 1869, Japan, for seven hundred years, had always had two sovereigns at the same time: one the ideal and secluded monarch,—the Mikado;

THE SHOGUN'S TOMB.

NEAR ENOSHIMA.

the other, the actual regent, known as the Shogun. Bearing this fact in mind we reached the summit of the staircase. Before us was a portal of black bronze, inscribed with Sanskrit characters in gold. Behind it was a small enclosure, surrounded by a massive wall. Only two dragon-headed dogs were stationed here as guardians; but no one dares set foot within the sacred area,—none save a priest may pass beneath the low-browed arch. But, standing on the steps, we obtained at least a glimpse of what is here enshrined. It is the tomb of Ieyasu, the most powerful military ruler of Japan. It is a simple cylinder of bronze, six feet in height, the roof of which curves upward like a miniature pagoda. In

NEGLECTED SHRINES.

front, upon a pedestal of stone, are the Japanese emblems of
immortality.   Here, then, the mightiest of the Shoguns
rests, in death exalted, as in life, above his subjects.   It is
an awe-inspiring burial-place.   Above him wave, like funeral
plumes, majestic cryptomerias; beneath him are the temples
where his spirit is adored; while, close beside him, in a

deep ravine,
the mountain
torrent moans
an endless re-
quiem.

Yet it was
when we left
the Shogun's
grave, and came
down through
the forest by
that foaming
stream, that we
best appreciat-
ed the grandeur
and sublimity
of Nikko.   No-
where in the
world, not even
on the Alham-

A MOUNTAIN TORRENT.

bra hill, have I been so profoundly moved and thoroughly
enchanted by a walk as by the one which winds about the
sacred mountain of Japan.   For miles above and around us
stretched a cryptomerian cathedral, whose columns were the
colossal trees, whose stained glass was the autumnal foliage,
whose altar-covering was the green velvet of the forest, whose
surpliced choristers were the white-robed and sweet-voiced
rivers and cascades.   One may well liken it to a cathedral,

for its shadowy expanse is tenanted by countless rustic monuments and altars. Most of them looked abandoned both by
gods and men; yet, here and there, we saw that worshipers

A CRYPTOMERIAN CATHEDRAL.

had not forgotten them entirely, since fragrant flowers lay
upon the thresholds of the few.

Lingering among these moss-grown emblems of an ancient
faith, and treading pathways deepened by the feet of millions
long since turned to dust, I shall never forget the impression
made upon me. I felt that I was assisting at the last hours

THE SACRED GROVE.

of a great relig- ion. " Young Japan " has no more use for these ances- tral shrines. It guards them merely as his- toric souvenirs: its faith in them is gone. In one sense, I was glad of this; but in another, I ex- perienced here a feeling of re-

gret. It seemed to me that this was earth's last strong- hold of romantic paganism, and that its life was ebbing fast.

THE LAST STRONGHOLD OF ROMANTIC PAGANISM.

Its sylvan gods, its nymphs and dryads of the hills, had left
these immemorial shrines; and I could easily fancy that the
drops of rain which fell that day from these old trees were in
reality Nature's tears of grief that Pan was dying.   Another
generation, and he will be dead.

JAPAN

II

JAPAN

THE most important dramas of the coming century will probably be enacted on the shores of the Pacific. Neither the European coast, nor yet our own, can now materially change; but over the mightiest ocean on our globe new constellations have arisen. Another Oriental horoscope must now be cast. Dormant so long, the East is re-awakening from her sleep of ages. Russia, the grim Colossus of the North,—facing, Janus-like, both east and west,—is making there a depot for her navy. Meantime she pushes on by day and by night her trans-Siberian railway, whose bars of steel will soon unite the Baltic and Pacific and revolutionize the commerce of the world. In the Northern Pacific, England and France have interests which are steadily increasing. Southward, Australia, and New Zealand too, must be considered carefully in any forecast of the future. Last, but not least, our own Pacific coast, with its magnificent shore-front of California and Alaska, and the boundless possibilities of Puget Sound, will fifty years hence have enormous interests

PRINCE ITO.

at stake. Meanwhile, Japan, central to all these various lands,
keen, bold, and active, both in war and peace, has suddenly
surpassed all records in her wonderful development, and even
now can almost keep step with the great Western Powers.

In 1892, the writer visited the Mikado's empire, and on
his return spoke enthusiastically of its people. But what he
said of China was precisely the reverse. On this account,
some thought that he exaggerated the virtues of the one and
the vices of the other. But the events of 1895 verified his
words. China has sunk still lower in the estimation of mankind, while Japan has risen far above the expectations of
her warmest friends. In fact, Japan, in many ways, is now
the most interesting country in the world. She is the pio-
neer of progress in the Orient. Consider her amazing growth

A DISTANT MARKET FOR CONNECTICUT CLOCKS.

in manufactures. By these she may ere long control the
commerce of the entire East. Look at her admirable schools
and universities. They can be favorably compared with not
a few in Europe. Think of her government, which in less

than twenty-five years has achieved what it took Europe centuries to accomplish,—to rid herself of feudalism and become
a constitutional monarchy. Regard her army, which accomplished marvels in the recent war; and her navy, which
elicited the admira-
tion of the world.

THE EDWIN BOOTH OF JAPAN.

In all these re-
spects we find a na-
tional transforma-
tion, which in rapid-
ity at least has had
no parallel in his-
tory. It is, then,
this extraordinary
land, which has a
long and brilliant
past, and is appar-
ently to have a still
more brilliant future,
that we are now to
explore still farther.

However novel
and attractive the
cities of the Mikado's empire may be, it is from traveling
through the country of Japan that one derives the greatest
pleasure and instruction. For it is not what Japan has bor-
rowed from the western world that most delights the foreign
tourist. On the contrary, the more he sees of their artistic,
happy, natural life, away from foreign contact, the better he
likes it.

It was on a beautiful October morning, that, leaving
cities and railways for a time behind us, we began our journey through a few of the Mikado's provinces. Seating ourselves in jinrikishas, we dashed across a little bridge and up

a mountain gorge which led to Miyanóshita.   There are few
things more thoroughly delightful than traveling through a
mountainous country in a carriage or on horseback.   On
a former trip I had thought that nothing could approach
in pleasure this mode of traveling in Norway.   But here
it proved fully as enjoyable.   It is true, the grandeur of
Norwegian scenery is not met with in Japan; but, on the
other hand,   the charming
novelty of
every-

thing
one sees,
makes such
excursions peerless in the traveler's memory.

APPROACHING MIYANÓSHITA.

At first, our road was an embowered lane winding along
a mountain-side, green to the summit with luxuriant foliage.
There was no parapet along the edge, as on the mountain
roads of Switzerland; but, as a reassuring compensation, we
had no horses here to back or shy or roll us down the
precipices.   The steeds that drew us up the narrow path were
copper-colored athletes, driven tandem, and without need of
rein or whip.   On, on they went with ceaseless energy, their

splendid mus-
cles working
like machinery.
Insensible to
fatigue, they
laughed and
talked inces-
santly, asking
only one favor
of their drivers,
—that of being
allowed to re-
duce their cloth-

A JAPANESE VILLAGE NEAR MIYANÓSHITA.

ing to the scantiest limits. Below us, as we rode along, was
an impetuous stream, which lured from time to time adven-
turous waterfalls to join its course. We halted to admire
one of these at our leisure. Its special charm was not its
height, though it descends several hundred feet: it was the

A BIT OF JAPAN.

wealth of col-
ored foliage
that made for
it a frame of
green and gold.
A little to the
left, an open-
ing in the trees
revealed a tiny
shrine, and in
the foreground
stood an aged
priest, who had
stopped to gaze
in wonder at
such strange

RURAL SCENERY IN JAPAN.

intruders. What pictures thus disclose themselves at every turn throughout this marvelous country! Anywhere else you would pronounce them stage effects— the cataracts which resemble tangled skeins of silken floss; the miniature pagodas interspersed among the trees; and, brightening all with life and color, the Japanese women

with their brilliant sashes, as if the vanished nymphs and dryads of the place had now assumed material shapes, intending to be worshiped somehow, even by the skeptics.

Yet this is what one sees

A MOUNTAIN STREAM.

A JAPANESE FAIR.

continually in Japan. What would in other lands seem artificial, is here only natural. Accordingly, the charm of Japanese scenery is enhanced by the surroundings given it by
man. Picturesque figures, clad in robes as multicolored as
the trees themselves; bridges, temples, and pagodas, often
as brilliant as the autumnal leaves around them—these make

A JAPANESE BRIDGE.

the landscapes irresistibly
attractive, as if both man
and Nature had agreed to wear at the same time their holi-
day attire. One feels that he is traveling through a land
where Nature is adored, where animals are kindly treated,
and where such pleasing and poetic myths as we associate
only with ancient Greece and Rome are still believed by

A FARMER IN HIS WORKING SUIT.

many faithful souls, and make each forest the abode of rural deities and every mountain rivulet a place of prayer.

As we moved farther up the valley, we found at every turn some new source of enjoyment; first, in the vivid foliage, which made the mountains seem like huge bouquets of ferns; then, in the silvery stream whose voice would shout a welcome to us as it hurried on; and lastly, in the little Japanese inns, along whose carved-wood balconies were hung red paper lanterns, that glowed at night like monster rubies, and gave to the whole scene that charmingly unreal, or theatrical effect, so characteristic of Japan.

Seeing some buildings on the opposite bank, we asked: "How do you cross here from shore to shore? Boats surely are not possible; nor are there

A RUSTIC BRIDGE.

any bridges, unless — but certainly those tiny structures
yonder, stretched like a spider's web across the flood, cannot be bridges!'' Yet closer scrutiny revealed the fact that
they are really used as a means of transportation. Long
poles of bamboo, bound about with reeds, and supported in
the centre by a rough-hewn tripod,—such are the structures
often spanning mountain-torrents in Japan! If swept away,

A CHARACTERISTIC VIEW.

they can easily be replaced; and, while they last, the peasants
cross them fearlessly.

"But how about wagons, carriages, and horses?'' we
inquired, only to be again reminded, with a laugh, that no
provision need be made for them, for carriage-roads do not
yet exist in these mountain regions, and horses are almost
as rare as centaurs. In fact, one of the first things to impress
us in these rural districts was the absence of animals. We
saw no oxen, sheep, or donkeys, and only in rare instances a
pony. Japanese farmers hardly know what meat, milk, and

butter are, and when one recollects that they have never
eaten bread, and have no word for it in their language, one
naturally asks, "On what do they live?" Through our in-
terpreter, we questioned a young laborer who was returning
homeward from the fields in his everyday working-suit of
clothes. He was well-formed and looked well-nourished, like
most of his fellows, yet he assured us that only fish, rice, and
vegetables formed his diet. When, therefore, one considers
how much hard work the Japanese perform, and thinks of all

A JAPANESE MEAL.

the thousands here, who, in lieu of horses, haul heavy loads
of wood and stone, it cannot be denied that they derive from
their food quite as much strength as we do from ours. It is
true, doctors declare that Japanese food, while good for
peasants working in the open air, is bad for those who lead
a sedentary life. But is anything good for those who lead
a sedentary life?

"What," we inquired somewhat impatiently, "is the
meaning of this dearth of animal life,—here, where a million
acres on these verdant hills would give the best of pasturage

for cattle?" The explanation given us was a religious one; for the Buddhist faith declares that to destroy any living creature is a sin. This doctrine, through successive centuries, has had a great effect upon the people. It practically forbids them to eat meat. If the United States, therefore, should

A POSTMAN.

ever become Buddhistic, a colossal industry of the West would disappear. No doubt, in time, stock-farms will be established in Japan, as foreigners create a large demand for beef, butter, milk, and cream; but agricultural customs are always

GATHERING SEA FOOD.

slow to change. One might have supposed that catching fish would also have been prohibited by Buddhism, since that involves the sacrifice of life. But, as the waters around the Japanese islands fairly swarm with them, to have forbidden the people fish would have removed their staple article of diet, and caused a positive hatred for the new religion. It is probable, therefore, that the Buddhist priests knew (just as well as the Japanese fishermen) where to draw the line.

One day, as we were rolling through the country in jin-rikishas, we saw approaching us an extraordinary apparition.

HOTEL AT MIYANOSHITA.

" What is it," we exclaimed, " a winged Mercury, or a Coney Island bather rushing to the beach?"

"That is the letter-carrier," was the reply; "and the small waterproof paper bag at the end of his bamboo pole contains the mail."

In fact, where villages are not reached by a railroad, the old system of swift couriers still prevails. Let us not laugh, however, at Japan's postal-service. It was only started in

1871; but it is already extended over the entire country, with more than five thousand post-offices and postal savings-banks. In 1881, after only ten years' growth, it carried ninety-five million letters and postal-cards, and its rate of postage is the cheapest in the world. A country postman, it is true, is rather oddly dressed. One thinks, at first, perhaps. that he is wearing a gaily-colored

A TATTOOED MAN.

jersey. Not at all — his only garment is a cloth about the waist, with a kerchief around his head to keep the perspiration out of his eyes, and he has straw sandals on his feet. He is tattooed. It seems impossible, at a first glance, that such elaborate decoration is produced by sepia and vermilion

A POST-OFFICE.

alone, carefully pricked in with needles; nevertheless it is a fact. These brilliant hues are proof against the greatest amount of washing. A tattooed man could no more change his colors than could an

Ethiopian his skin or a leopard his spots.   In feudal times this style of ornamentation was resorted to by the Japanese for the same reason that their hideous masks were worn in

AT MIYANÓSHITA.

battle,— in order to inspire fear. Even now, although the custom is prohibited, some wonderful specimens of tattooing can be seen; and from actual observation we were forced to believe the statement that artists in that line are able to prick into the skin a fairly faithful likeness of the man himself, or perchance of a friend. Such workmen now complain that they have little opportunity to practice their profession.   Some patronage, however, still comes to them from youthful foreigners.   Two sons of the Prince of Wales, for example, as well as Prince George of Greece, have on their bodies specimens of this ornamentation; and if some travelers whom we met here could be induced to raise their sleeves they would display to their astonished friends one or two very pretty Japanese views,— "colored,"—though not "dissolving."

One of the first and most delightful halting-places in our trip across Japan was the hotel at Miyanóshita.   It is as dainty as a lacquered box, with floors, chairs, and balustrades as neat as wax and beautifully polished.   The rooms

RURAL SCENERY.

are furnished simply, but in European style; the food is specially prepared for foreigners; and in cold weather the corridors can be enclosed in glass. What wonder, then, that tourists resort to Miyanóshita? For, in addition to its good hotel, it has the best of mountain air and delightful hot baths from a natural spring, and is a starting-point for many notable excursions. On most of these, however, jinrikishas cannot be used.

From this point on, the beaten roads are left, and only narrow paths ascend the hills. Hence, on the morning after our arrival, we found ourselves confronted by the most novel style of conveyance we had thus far seen. "What under heaven is this?" I cried, as I caught sight of it. "Must I get into this thing, and haven't you any blankets for these horses?"

My friend sat down upon a rock and vowed he would not go. "Give me a jinrikisha," he moaned; "I'd rather be once more a baby-jumper in my little carriage than a mere stone in a sling, as you will be in that!" He finally compromised on an arm-chair, hung on bamboo poles and carried by four men; but I resolved to give this vehicle a thorough trial.

A KAGO.

So crawling in, like a dog into its basket, I crossed my legs after the fashion of a Turk who had fallen over backward,

and told my well-groomed steeds to go ahead. The unique
and novel instrument of torture to which I thus subjected
myself is called a "kago." It is a shallow basket, suspended from a bamboo pole, on
which it swings irregularly
like an erratic pendulum.
Two men take this upon
their shoulders, while a third
follows as a sub-
stitute; for

they change
places usually
every fifteen minutes.
Mine changed every five.
The man who invented
the iron cage, within
which the unhappy pris-
oner could neither stand
up nor lie down, must
have heard of a Japanese

1. A RAIN-COAT.   2. AMONG THE FLOWERS.   3. A KAGO.

kago. The basket is too near the pole to let the occupant
sit erect, and much too short for him to extend his feet
without giving the bearer in front a violent prod in the small
of the back. After many frantic experiments, I found that

the easiest fashion of kago-riding was to lie upon my side, my
head lolling about in one direction, and my feet in the other.
Even then, the lower half of my body kept falling asleep, and
I was frequently obliged to get out and walk, to avoid curv-
ature of the spine. Yet, incredible though it seems, Japanese

SWINGING LIKE A PENDULUM.

women often travel by these kagos. They certainly looked a
thousand times more comfortable than I felt; but then, the
Japanese are short, and, moreover, are used to bending up
their limbs like knife-blades when they seat themselves.

On a broad road, one experiences no sense of danger in
these swinging cars; but, once in a while, when I was being

carried thus along a path two feet in width,—a mountain graz-
ing my right elbow, and a ravine one thousand feet in depth
just under my left shoulder-blade, I used to wonder just what
would happen if one of these men should stumble; or if,
becoming weary of their load, they should suddenly shoot
me outward into space like a stone from a catapult.   I pru-
dently kept on good terms with my kago-men, and never

HUMAN PONIES.

refused them when they asked the privilege of halting to
take a smoke.

Almost everything in Japan is small; nor is a Japanese
pipe an exception to the rule.   It is about as large as a lead-
pencil with a child's thimble at the end.   Three whiffs are
all that any man can take from them, and the wad of tobacco
thus consumed is just about the size of a two-grain quinine
pill.   Hence, the long inhalations of our smokers, the drooping backward of the head, the languid lifting of the eyes to
watch the rings of perfumed smoke float lazily away,—all

these are un-
known to the
Japanese. With
them, — three
little puffs, and
all is over. This
seems, however,
to satisfy them
completely, and
with the air of
one who has
dined well, they
knock the ashes
from the tiny
thimbles, and

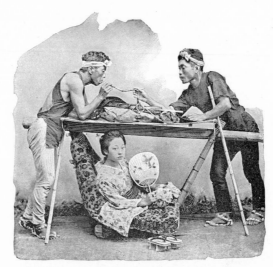

STOPPING FOR A SMOKE.

resume their march. After about four hours of this kago-
riding we reached the summit of a mountain pass, called
Otemetoge. From this point a glorious vista met our gaze.

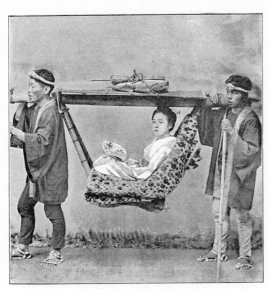

A JAPANESE LADY EN ROUTE.

Behind us, in
the distance, lay
Miyanóshita and
its neighboring
villages, resem-
bling a group
of islands in an
ocean of green
foliage. Far
off upon the
heights a line of
sunlit buildings
gleamed like
whitecaps on a
bright-green sea.
Nearer, and al-

most at our feet, some objects glittering in the noonday light attracted our attention; and these, examined through a field-glass, proved to be a foaming mountain stream and silvery cascade.   At first we hardly dared to look on the other side

FUJI-YAMA.

of the pass, lest we should experience disappointment.   But fortune favored us.   The sky was clear; and gazing eagerly toward the west, we saw, directly opposite our point of observation, the grand old sacred mountain of Japan,—the world-renowned Fuji-yama.

It made me fairly catch my breath to look for the first time upon this noble peak, whose form had been portrayed on almost every specimen of Japanese art that I had seen from childhood.   I felt as if I had been ushered into the presence of some mighty sovereign, whose name and deeds and splendid court had from my earliest years called forth my admiration.   A score of interesting traits render a study of this mountain valuable.   It is, in the first place, a volcano,—the tallest of those fiery furnaces whose devastations cast a lurid light along the path of Japanese history.   Its last eruption was in 1707, when all the plain around its base was buried deep with cinders, and ashes fell fifty miles away. Yet even now, although no wreath of smoke surrounds its brow, it sends forth steam through several apertures, much as a captive serpent hisses though its fangs are drawn. The little spur upon its southern slope is due to the last eruption. Before that, both of its curving sides were perfectly symmetrical.

The ascent of Fuji involves a long, hard climb for weary miles through lava-ashes, sometimes ankle-deep. The violence of the wind on certain portions of the mountain is proverbial, and by some travelers has been described as so appalling that they were fearful lest some furious blast might blow them into space and scatter their remains over a dozen provinces.

THE SACRED PEAK.

One cannot wonder that the Japanese have always deemed this mountain sacred. A perfect, silver-crested pyramid, over twelve thousand feet in height, rising in one majestic sweep from sea to sky; changing its color constantly from dawn to

APPROACH TO A SHRINE.

dusk, like some officiating priest, a mediator between God and man, assuming consecrated robes of purple, orange, violet, green, and gold, — how could man help regarding it as a glorious shrine inhabited by Deity itself? To its mighty base, as to some incense-burning altar, more than ten thousand reverent pilgrims annually come to make the arduous ascent; and to relieve their hardships, "rest-houses" have been built at intervals along the path, while, even on the summit, the three entrances to the volcano's crater, which is four hundred feet deep, are marked by sacred gateways. Most of these pilgrims

THE GOD OF WIND.

MENDICANT PILGRIMS.

wear upon their shoulders the garments almost universally worn in stormy weather by the Japanese peasants, — a kind of waterproof, made of straw or grass, to shed the rain and snow. These vary from a finely-plaited matting to the cheaper, rougher grades, which make the wearer's back look like the roof of a thatched cottage. Upon their heads are hats of split bamboo or straw, that bear a comical resemblance to enormous mushrooms, and serve as sunshades or umbrellas, according to the condition of the weather. We met such pilgrims everywhere throughout Japan. At least a hundred thousand people thus become, in summer-time, religious tramps, and make their

THE PILGRIM GARB.

STATUE OF JIZO.

way to sacred islands, holy mountain-tops, and shrines whose names would fill a lengthy catalogue.

Many of these itinerant worshipers solicit alms to help them on their way; but there are also associations of these pilgrims, whose members pay one cent a month into a common treasury. From such a tax as that, however, the treasury never

CROSSING THE
TEN-PROVINCE PASS.

VILLAGE STREET.

A LOVELY WALK NEAR HAKONE.

becomes congested, and hence the number of those who travel is necessarily limited. When, therefore, the pilgrim season opens, a certain number of the wanderers, chosen by lot, visit the shrines and represent those whose circumstances compel them to remain at home. These pilgrimages, it is said, are on the wane, but they are still popular. Only five

APPROACH TO THE
TEMPLE AT NARA.

years ago, at the festival of one famous shrine, twenty-one
thousand people alighted in two days at a country railway
station where the daily average is three hundred and fifty;
and to another sacred shrine about two hundred and fifty
thousand pilgrims annually come.

Another charming excursion in Japan led us across the
" Ten-province pass" to Atami on the southern coast. Of
course it had to be made in chairs or kagos; but such slight

ON THE SHORE OF HAKONE LAKE.

hardships sink to insignificance when one recalls delightful
days spent in enjoying lovely scenery, inhaling pure, invigorating air, and riding over mountain-paths on which the
sunlight, filtering through the trees, traced tremulous mosaics
of alternate light and shade.

Occasionally on this journey we came upon the sculptured effigy of some protecting deity. We were especially
impressed by one that was colossal in dimensions, and had
been carved laboriously from the natural cliff eleven hundred
years before. It represents the Buddhist god, Jizo, who is

the especial guardian of travelers and little children. Around
the base of this extraordinary figure were heaps of pebbles
which had been placed there, one by one, by wayfarers for
centuries. This custom originated in one of the most singular myths which religion has ever produced, and is a striking
proof of the fondness of the Japanese for children. Upon
the banks of the river, in the lower world, is said to live a
demon who catches little children as they try to cross, and

THE MIKADO'S PALACE, HAKONE.

makes them work for him at his eternal task of piling stones
upon the shore. Every pebble laid at the statue's feet is
thought to lighten the burden of some little one below!
Smilingly yielding to the influence of this pathetic super-
stition, we ourselves left some pebbles, and then moved
onward down the mountain side, in the same path pursued by
all the thousands who had here preceded us, like little boats
upon the stream of Time.

Presently a sudden turn revealed to us Hakone Lake,—a
lovely sheet of water surrounded by densely wooded hills.

ATAMI.

This is a summer resort that rivals even Miyanóshita in popularity. The air is delightfully invigorating here, twenty-four hundred feet above the sea, and in the hot season, not only are all the Japanese tea-houses filled with guests, but families from Tokio and Yokohama rent all the available cottages around the lake. To some extent, indeed, this region has imperial patronage, for, on a pretty hill which overlooks the water, is a palace built for the Mikado. It must be said, however, that he has never occupied it, since he rarely leaves his residence in Tokio, but we were told that the Crown Prince, a lad of fourteen, had been here several times. In almost every other country in the world the public is now permitted

THE GEYSER AT ATAMI.

to enter the abodes of royalty when their distinguished occupants are absent; but not so here. These palace doors are closed inexorably to all travelers. We were not allowed even to step within the grounds.

At length, descending to the level of the sea, our faithful bearers brought us to Atami—a pretty town, famous for the manufacture of that Japanese paper which seemed to me one of the most astonishing products of the country. It is so fine

BY LAKE HAKONE.

and soft that it is used for handkerchiefs and napkins, and takes the place of lint in surgery; yet is so firm that it is manufactured into lantern screens, brooms, air-cushions, and umbrellas. Torn into strips, it also takes the place of string, while all the inner walls of Japanese houses consist of screens of paper, divided into squares, like panes of glass.

As we were one day walking through Atami, a sudden outburst of steam, on the other side of a fence, came very near stampeding our entire party. When we recovered sufficient breath to ask the cause of the explosion, we learned that

A MIXTURE OF STYLES.

it was occasioned by a small geyser, which has a species of convulsion every four hours, and each time pours out sulphurous vapor for a space of fifteen minutes.

It would appear that the people of Atami are living on the lid of a volcanic tea-kettle, but evidently they have no fear. They have enclosed the geyser with a fence like a wild animal in a cage, and close beside it is a sanitarium, where patients with diseases of the throat and lungs inhale the steam. It may be an excellent place for sufferers from pulmonary troubles, but we concluded that nervous occupants of this retreat must feel like the traditional darky on the safety-valve of a Mississippi steamboat.

The old-style doctors of Japan are still in vogue in certain rural districts, though they are being rapidly superseded by the young practitioners who have received a medical education in Europe or America. With the old Japanese physicians a favorite mode of cure was sticking a long needle into the part of the body supposed to be diseased. Another universal panacea was branding the body with a burning weed called *moxa*. This was prescribed for troubles as unlike as rheuma-

A JAPANESE DOCTOR OF THE OLD STYLE.

A JAPANESE LADY.

tism and toothache. Women, at certain critical moments in their lives, were thought to be relieved by having the little toe of their right foot burned three times. We often noticed scars upon the naked backs and limbs of our jinrikishà men, and learned that they had been produced by this strange medical treatment.

In traveling through the rural districts of Japan, the tourist soon becomes accustomed to the peasant's lack of clothing. It is not the exception here to be undressed—it is the rule.

Even in the streets of Tokio one will behold, on rainy days, thousands of men wearing neither trousers nor stockings, walking about with tucked-up clothes and long white limbs, which gives them the appearance of

DRESS AND UNDRESS.

storks upon a river-bank. Even those who have adopted the European dress will frequently, on a muddy day, practice economy by discarding their trousers, and, unconscious of any incongruity, will take their "constitutional" on wooden clogs, with bare legs and feet, though having the upper part of their bodies covered with a frock-coat and a Derby hat!

Among these scantily-clad people one often sees a somewhat better dressed but melancholy man, who, with his downcast eyes and shaven head, appears to have lost his friends together with his hair. He represents a useful class

A MASSEUR.

of people in Japan — the *masseurs*, or professional manipulators of the body. One should not hastily conclude that he is smoking. It is true, the article between his lips is usually a pipe, but it is not the kind that holds tobacco. It is a reed-like instrument, on which he blows two plaintive notes to advertise his presence. In every Japanese town we always heard at night the mournful call of the *masseur*. The laughter which their appearance at first provokes, gives place to pity when one learns that nearly all of these men are blind. It is a calling which, notwithstanding their infirmity, they can follow, and they are said to be adepts at it.

To appreciate a Japanese *masseur*, it is necessary to see one of them at work. This, it is true, is more than he himself can do, since he is blind; but our pity is soon diverted from

MASSAGE.

JAPANESE COIFFURE.

him to the person he is treating, not so much because of the pinching to which he subjects his victim as on account of the pillow on which the patient's head reclines. It makes one think of Anne Boleyn or Mary Stuart, with their necks upon the fatal block; for a Japanese pillow is a wedge-shaped piece of wood, about a foot in length, on top of which is tied a wad of cloth, about the size of a Bologna sausage. To try to sleep with the neck supported in this fashion would seem to most Americans as hopeless as to woo slumber with a fence-rail for a pillow. One shudders to consider the discomfort, under these conditions, of turning over in bed, and trying to locate the neck on such a diminutive support. Yet, after all, we are creatures of habit, and forty million people in Japan use just such pillows every night, without suffering from insomnia. It is even claimed that Japanese women delight in them, since they do not disarrange the hair. Nor does this appear strange, when one scrutinizes their methods of coiffure. They are something marvelous. The

A JAPANESE PILLOW.

IN THE BOUDOIR.

hair of Japanese women is, with few exceptions, as black as ebony, and very abundant. More-over, it is usually pro-fusely oiled, and glis-tens like a raven's wing. Through these polished tresses are invariably drawn hairpins of gold, strings of coral, or orna-ments of tortoise-shell. But as to how the la-dies of Japan produce in their coiffures their black crescendos and diminuendos, their sharp staccato puffs and portamento water-falls, the writer dares not hazard a conjecture. Yet of one thing we may be sure: if we were to venture into a Japanese lady's boudoir, we should find that help is needed to produce them. The toilette-stand and looking-glass might seem to us a trifle low; but we must bear in mind that Japanese domes-tic life is regulat-ed by a level three feet lower than our own: in other words, where we use chairs,

THE LAST TOUCHES.

they seat themselves on the floor. This furnished us a key to much that hitherto had seemed puzzling in their habits. Whether a thing be sensible or not depends upon the point of view,— in this case, the height at which we seat ourselves. Once regard an exquisitely clean floor of cushioned matting as an immense divan, and taking off our muddy boots becomes a matter of course; and tables and lamps and mirrors will be placed at a height adapted to our needs.

When a foreigner beholds for the first time a Japanese lady seated on her heels, as is the custom, he fancies that she has the small of her back supported by an enormous cushion. But when he subsequently sees this lady walking down the street, attended by her maid, he perceives that what appeared to him a sofa-pillow is really a regular part of her costume.

THE OBI.

It is a heavy silken sash, extremely long and often very elegant, which keeps the robe itself in place. This *obi*, as it is called, is the most precious article of a Japanese lady's wardrobe. Its usual length is fourteen feet, and when its material is silk or gold brocade it will be seen that it has some value. These sashes exhibit, of course, a great variety of color, and one can scarcely find a prettier sight than that of several well-dressed Japanese ladies, grouped together in the vivid sunlight. They look as radiant and attractive as a bouquet of flowers.

A JAPANESE BEAUTY.

American ladies who have tried the Japanese dress say that the tying of the *obi* is extremely difficult. But here, as in the art of hair-dressing, a lady's maid is almost indispensable. The bow, although arranged in different styles, is always worn behind, thus spoiling, in some measure, the outline of the form. When a Japanese lady becomes a widow, she makes no change in the position of the *obi*, unless she wishes publicly to announce that she will never marry again. In that case, it is said, she ties the bow in front. Whether this wards off all proposals may be doubted; but gossip relates that, once in a while, the

widow comes to look at life a little differently, and then the bow works gradually round again to its original position.

Japanese ladies make a serious mistake when they exchange their national style of dress for that of foreigners, for, as a rule, their charm and beauty leave them when they appear in European garments. On two occasions we saw some thus arrayed, and

TYING THE OBI.

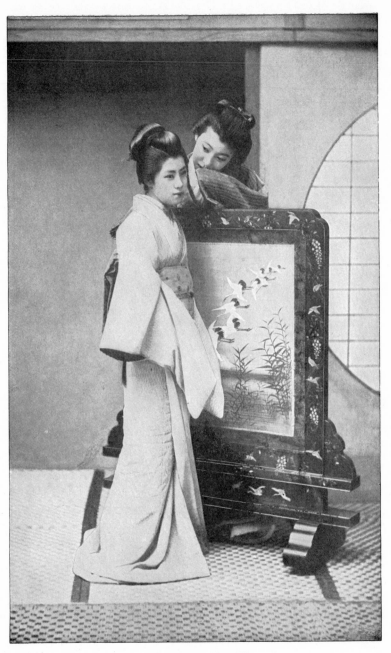

FRIENDS IN COUNCIL.

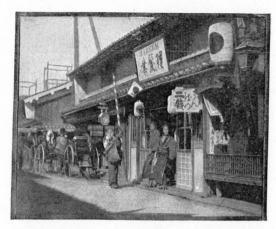

A JAPANESE SHOP.

the effect was painful. If most of them had put on each other's dresses by mistake, they would have looked about as well; and in the absence of corsets their little figures seemed as much out of place as children in their mother's wrappers.

Some years ago a letter signed by Mrs. Cleveland and many other prominent women of America was addressed to their sisters in Japan, urging them not to risk their health and comfort by adopting European dress. It was of little avail. The die was cast. In 1885 the Japanese Empress and her

A BOAT-RIDE IN JAPAN.

suite appeared for the last time in public in the tasteful costumes of the past.   Since then, the order has gone forth that

all ladies who
present them-
selves at court
must do so in
European dress;
and it is to be
feared that, ere
a score of years
have passed, the
lovely and appro-
priate robes of
old Japan will
have disappeared

GEISHA GIRLS.

forever.   Until quite recently, the universal rule for Japanese
women, when they married, was to shave their eyebrows, pull

out their eye-
lashes, and stain
their teeth jet
black.   Even
the present em-
press did these
things at her
marriage.   The
idea seems to
have been to
make them-
selves look hid-
eous, so as to
have no more
admirers, de-

A DANCING GIRL.

spite the fact that the average husband, as we all know, ap-
preciates his wife better if he perceives that other men are

aware of her attractions. But under the new *régime* this sad disfigurement is rapidly disappearing, and at present the younger ladies of Japan, at least, show rows of pearly teeth when laughter parts their lips.

The richest toilettes that we saw in the land of the Mikado were worn by *geisha* girls, without whom Japanese festivals are incomplete. Some of these dainty creatures form an orchestra while others dance. Their instruments of sound

A TEA-HOUSE.

(one can hardly call them instruments of music) consist usually of two kinds of drums and a long, three-stringed banjo, called the *samisen*. Sometimes a flute also is used. We frequently disputed as to which of these was the least excruciating, but on the whole we preferred the drums. When to this combination a human voice was added, our teeth were set on edge.

Young as they look, these *geishas* are professionals, and training-schools exist in Tokio and Kioto, where they are sometimes taught when only seven years of age. A Japanese dancing-girl forms a charming picture. Her long *kimono* of the

A JAPANESE FAMILY MOVING.

richest silk is beautifully embroidered with such a wealth of lovely flowers, that she herself resembles a bouquet in motion. Her broad *obi* is of the heaviest crape, and falls upon a petticoat of gorgeous color. Black lacquered sandals half conceal her tiny, white-socked feet, and in each hand she holds a decorated fan. Do not expect from her the slightest approach to Lottie Collins. The dance of "Ta-ra-ra-boom-de-ay," performed by a *geisha* girl, would make a subject of the Mikado, if he were unprepared for it, faint away. Nor will the spectator see the least exposure of her personal charms. For, strangely enough, the Japanese, who will at other times dispense with all the clothing possible, conceal a dancer's form with rigid severity. There is not much expression in these dancers' faces. One feels that they are not women, but girls to whom intense emotions

ON THE JAPANESE COAST.

are as yet unknown. They merely represent in graceful pan-
tomime some song or story, flitting about like pretty butter-
flies, or swaying back and forth like flowers in a summer breeze.

Leaving Atami, we had a charming ride of seven miles
beside the ocean. The road (which may be called the Japanese Cornice) is passable for jinrikishas; and while on one
side we looked off upon the Pacific, on the other we found that

LOVERS OF NATURE AND ART.

every valley had a background of well-rounded mountains,
covered with verdure soft as velvet, from which at intervals a
stream of crystal water rushed to meet the sea. The scenery
of Japan may not be grand, but for a charming combination
of the elements which make a country beautiful, enlivened
constantly by natives in their novel occupations, the seven-
mile drive from old Atami can hardly be surpassed.

Moreover, the people, as we met them on these journeys,
pleased us greatly. They were invariably courteous and
gentle in their manners, and no boorishness was visible, even

among the lower classes. They always seemed to be good-
natured. However stormy the weather, however heavy the
load, however bad the roads, we never heard a Japanese complain, nor saw one in a bad humor. If the foreigner becomes
angry with them, they laugh as if he were making himself

A JAPANESE AT PRAYER.

ridiculous; and presently he feels that they are right, and that
violent anger is in truth absurd.

Yet, just as beneath the smiling landscapes of Japan still
lurk the terrible volcanic forces of destruction, so underneath
the sunny dispositions of the Japanese are all the character-
istics of the warrior. Their history has thoroughly established that they are a manly, patriotic, martial race. Their
gentleness, therefore, comes not from servility, but is the
product of inborn courtesy and refinement.

The Japanese are naturally of a happy disposition. A
smile illumines every face. Apparently their past has no
regrets, their present no annoyances, their future no alarms.

THE GUARDIAN OF TRAVELERS AND LITTLE CHILDREN.

They love the beautiful in nature and in art. They live simply; and how much that means! Their wants are few. The houses of the wealthy do not differ much from those of the poor. Hence life for them is free from almost all those harrowing cares and worriments which sometimes make existence in the Occident a long, incessant struggle to keep up appearances. If they are sad, they seldom show their sadness in public. They evidently believe with the poet:

> "Laugh, and the world laughs with you;
> Weep, and you weep alone."

In some provinces of Japan, when a new bridge is opened, not the richest, but the happiest, persons in the community are chosen to pass over it first, as a favorable omen.

Strange as it may appear, however, these qualities of the Japanese have been regarded by some travelers as faults. A tourist once solemnly remarked to me: "The great trouble with the Japanese is that they are too happy."

"What!" I exclaimed, "can any one be too happy in this world?"

"Certainly," was the reply; "the Japanese are too light-hearted to

A JAPANESE HEARSE.

learn with advantage the lessons of adversity. If a calamity befalls them, they often smile and say, 'Well, it can't be helped,' and then try to think no more about it. Worst of all," he continued, "they do not worry about the future, but actually meet death fearlessly and calmly."

"My friend," I answered, "if to enjoy as much as possible this world that God has given us, if to smile bravely in
adversity, and if to die without fear, are faults, it would be
well if many other people possessed them, too.   You re-

mind me of the
old lady in New
Hampshire, who
exclaimed sadly,
' The Universal-
ists tell us that
all men are to be
saved, but — we
hope for better
things!' "

In fact, a re-
markable char-
acteristic of the
Japanese is the
cheerful, almost
jovial, way they

A BARBER SHOP.

have of announcing a calamity.   An English resident of Japan
called our attention to this fact soon after our arrival, and our
experience confirmed his testimony.   Whether the cause be
nervousness or a dislike to give one pain, the fact remains
that the Japanese will often preface a bit of dreadful news
with laughter, or at least with a chuckle.   Thus, whenever
our guide called our attention to a funeral, his face would
wreathe itself in smiles.

Still more extraordinary was the manner of a barber in the
hotel at Yokohama.   As he was shaving me one morning,
after a moderate earthquake-shock the night before, he suddenly remarked, with what appeared to be a burst of unpre-
meditated merriment: "Oh, last night's shock was nothing.
Why, a few years ago, in Tokio, my father and mother were

killed outright by an earthquake (Ha! Ha!); the house fell
right on top of them (He! He!), and crushed them both to
death (Ha! Ha! Ha!)."

It is difficult to explain this peculiarity otherwise than by
supposing it to be a nervous mannerism; for, as a race, the
Japanese are very affectionate, and filial reverence is a religious duty.   In this instance I was so astonished at the man's
hilarity, that I very nearly fell out of his chair.   We thought
of this incident again, when, some weeks later, we found
ourselves in the Japanese province which had suffered most
from the calamitous earthquake of October, 1891.   Thousands of houses, we found, had been wrecked by that catas-

A RUINED VILLAGE.

trophe, and in one place the railway tracks had been vio-
lently bent and twisted, like a chain irregularly thrown upon
the ground.   The motion lasted less than a minute; but what
cannot an earthquake do in forty seconds?   There came one

SCATTERED BY AN EARTHQUAKE.

mighty shock,— and over an extent of many miles the buildings fell like packs of cards. Great blocks of solid masonry were tossed about like dice. Trees lay around like jackstraws. Large manufacturing towns were ruined. Thousands of husbands, wives, and children who, but an instant previous, had been happy at their work or play, were suddenly crushed by falling roofs, mangled by heavy timbers, buried alive in the *débris*, or burned to ashes by fires caused by overturned braziers. By chance we traveled through this region on the first anniversary of that great calamity, and many people, we were told, felt anxious till the day was over. But earthquakes in Japan, alas! are limited

TWISTED BY AN EARTHQUAKE.

to no special dates. Their visits are extremely numerous and quite impartial as to months and days. Our earth is said to be quieting down in its subterranean disturbances; but poor Japan still has no less than fifty-one volcanoes labeled "active," and experiences every year, on an average, five hundred seismic shocks, besides numerous destructive typhoons or hurricanes. Most of them are, of course, mere tremors;

EFFECT OF A TYPHOON AT KOBE.

but once in a while there comes a stroke that causes fearful devastation, as when in Tokio, in 1703, thirty-seven thousand lives were lost. Such terrible manifestations of volcanic power remind one of the more appalling scenes that must have been enacted here, when Nature brought these islands from the sea, pouring them from her fiery crucible.

In planning a journey through the interior of Japan, the tourist naturally inquires where and with what accommodation he is to spend the nights upon the trip. He need not have the least anxiety. In the four prominent cities,—Tokio, Yokohama, Kobe, and Kioto,— there are first-class hotels, with rooms and food adapted to the tastes of foreigners. In many smaller places, too, like Miyanóshita and Atami, the hotels, although simpler, are both comfortable and well-managed. One suffers no discomfort in any of these localities. But in the country villages (which need not be included in

HOTEL AT KOBE.

the traveler's route unless he so desires), he must adopt the Japanese mode of sleeping in a tea-house—that is to say, in a regular Japanese hotel.

As our jinrikishas drew up before one of these, we saw a pretty, modern building of two stories, adorned as usual with paper lanterns. At intervals, on the edge of every balcony, were tall, rectangular boxes reaching from floor to ceiling. These upright cases contain wooden shutters, about as large as the leaves of a dining-table, which are at night taken out, and pushed along in grooves, to make an outside wall for the entire house. When that is done, each balcony of course be-

comes an inside corridor. Thus every Japanese dwelling con- sists, as it were, of two houses, one within the other, enclosed in separate cases,— the in-

THREE OF A KIND.

side one of paper, the outer one of wood. As we alighted here, the landlord and his servants hurried out to greet us, dropped on their knees, and, with their hands spread out,

A TEA-HOUSE.

palms down- ward, and their foreheads al- most touching the floor, they bowed repeat- edly, like the "three little maids from school." What a contrast was here between the Orient and the Occident. Imagine a hotel clerk in America down upon his knees! In our hotels the traveler's first duty is to register his name. Here there is something even more

important to attend to, namely, removing his shoes. Off
they must come before he steps upon the delicate mattings
and the glistening floor, just as with us a muddy overshoe
would not be tolerated on a parlor carpet.   In fact, on entering the hall, one sees what in America would be called a hat-
rack, but which is here designed for holding shoes.

The tourist, therefore, should invariably carry with him in
Japan a pair of soft, felt slippers, for otherwise he will be fre-

A TEA-HOUSE VESTIBULE.

quently obliged
to walk about
in hotels, shops,
and temples,
with merely
stockings on his
feet.

In nearly all
Japanese dwell-
ings one usual-
ly finds, hung
in conspicuous
places, some
handsomely
framed mottoes
and proverbs,

much as in many of our own country houses we read upon
the walls such a comforting assurance as "The Lord will pro-
vide," or the melancholy conundrum "What is home without
a mother?"   To Occidental eyes, Japanese ideographs do not
appear beautiful.   They look like the meanderings of intoxicated flies that have been immersed in ink.   As for their
meaning, one motto was translated to us as signifying: "May
Buddha bless this house!"   Others were words of praise which
princely visitors had left; while not a few were epigrams or
proverbs, for which the Japanese are famous.   Some of them

WRITING A LETTER.

ran as follows: "The absent get farther away every day;" "Clever preacher, short sermon;" "A woman's tongue three

inches long can kill a man six feet high;" "Live under your own hat;" "Don't make a long call when the husband is not at home." And yet we send missionaries to Japan!

AT THE TEA-HOUSE DOOR.

With many bows and smiles the landlord of the tea-house led the way up a flight of exquisitely polished stairs, and showed us our apartments. We looked around us with astonishment, for no furniture was visible. The floor, it is true, was covered with fine matting, but, with that one exception, the rooms, which opened into each other, were as bare as

JAPANESE MOTTOES.

an unfurnished flat. Their number and extent depended largely on ourselves. Did we desire an entire story? We had but to push back the paper screens, and it was ours. Did we insist on having separate rooms? Close up the little screens again, and each could sleep in his own paper box,

exactly twelve feet square. Unfortunately there are no locks
upon these paper screens; hence, just as one is getting out of
bed in the morning, the whole side of his room will sometimes
disappear with the rapidity of a liberated Holland shade!
Moreover, Japanese servants, urged by curiosity, will often
poke a moistened finger through a square of paper, to study
foreign toilettes at their leisure. During the daytime, in the

INTERIOR OF A TEA-HOUSE.

summer, even the screens are removed, to give free access to
the breeze, and the house then becomes the empty skeleton
of its former self.

But what most puzzled us at first was where to hang our
clothes. There were no hooks upon the walls, there was not
even a table for our toilet articles. It seemed too bad to put
our coats and hair-brushes on the floor. But one must recollect
that Japanese floors are not like ours, since no boots ever
touch them. For native guests a beautiful, square, lacquered
box is usually provided, in which they lay the carefully folded

robes which they remove before retiring. To us, however, no limited receptacle like that was given. We had the unrestricted floor.

The beds in which we slept afforded us the most amusement. When bedtime comes in Japanese homes, quilts are brought out from a closet and spread upon the floor. Within

A JAPANESE BED.

five minutes all is ready for the night, and with the morning light they disappear again. Occasionally, in the larger teahouses, we, as foreigners, had special luxuries,—such as cotton sheets, a couch of seven comforters, instead of the usual two, and, for a bolster, an extra quilt rolled up as with a shawl-strap. Thus altogether, including what we used for coverings, our most luxurious couches in Japan consisted of from ten to a dozen comforters.

THE COMMON WASHSTAND IN A TEA-HOUSE.

We found some difficulty in getting sufficient sleep in Japanese tea-houses; not from the composition and arrangement of our beds, but from the noise about us, which seldom ceased before the hour of midnight, and always woke us with the dawn. Even our "summer hotels," with their distressingly thin partitions, are delightfully tranquil compared with the country inns of Japan. For sliding screens of paper are practically no barrier at all to sound, and, as if that were not sufficiently aggravating, these paper walls rarely reach the top of the room, but leave a ventilating space of a foot or two, through which the mingled snoring, prayers, and

JAPANESE TEA-HOUSE.

conversation of the guests, and the matutinal clatter of the servants, roll and reverberate like distant thunder.

The morning after my arrival, I pushed aside a screen with my forefinger, and lo! half of my room

CARRYING TEA FROM THE FIELD.

stood open to the rising sun. Descending to the courtyard, I beheld a Japanese servant hurrying toward me on her wooden clogs, to give me tea.

What shall be said of these attractive little waitresses, who make the dullest tea-house gay with laughter, brighten the darkest day with brilliant colors, and sweeten every tea-cup with a smile? They are not usually beautiful, or even womanly, in the sense of being dignified. They rather seem like well-developed school-girls, just sobered down enough to wear long dresses, but perfectly unable to refrain at times from screams of merriment. Yet search the world through, and where will you find servants such as these? From the first moment when they fall upon their knees and bow their foreheads to the floor, till the last instant, when they troop around

BRINGING TEA.

the door to call to you their musical word for farewell,— "*Sayonara,*"— they seem to be the daintiest, happiest, and

PLAYING GAMES.

most obliging specimens of humanity that walk the earth. We were particularly pleased with one agreeable trait of all these Japanese girls — their exquisitely clean and well-shaped hands. One would, of course, expect them to be small, for delicate frames are a characteristic of the race, but almost without exception the hands of all the waitresses who served us in Japan looked as if they had just emerged from a hot bath, and had been manicured besides. "A trifle," some would say, but, after all, such trifles help to make perfection. When one has traveled through a country for two months, and from one end of it to the other has seen pretty,

TWO MODES OF TRAVEL IN JAPAN.

well-kept hands extended to him fifty times a day, he feels respect and admiration for a race so neat and delicate to their finger-tips. The Japanese, according to our Occidental standard, may not have much godliness, but they possess what comes next to it—personal cleanliness. And I am sure that, at any time, I would rather associate with a nice, wholesome sinner than with an uncleanly saint!

It was while we were taking our breakfast here, that we beheld, in a neighboring room, a lady being served with tea

by her domestic, who was approaching her mistress on her knees. Nothing amazed us more than this, for in the United
States these positions are usually reversed. In free America it is the lady who, figuratively speaking, has to "go down on her knees" before her cook. When we consider the serious

DOMESTIC ETIQUETTE.

drawbacks to domestic happiness and comfort, occasioned by the insolence and inefficiency of servants in America, who, as a rule, are better lodged, clothed, and fed than any other class of laborers in the world, one questions if in this, and many other respects, Japan will be improved by contact with the Occident.

What Moscow is to the Russians, Kioto is to the Japanese, their present capital, Tokio, corresponding rather to St. Petersburg. Kioto is the ancient cap-

A STREET IN KIOTO.

ital,— the sacred city of the empire,—hallowed by countless shrines and endeared by centuries of classic memories. It was for a thousand years the home of the Mikado, and is still the centre of old Japanese art.   Here also, till the revolution of 1869, lived many nobles of the highest rank, together with distinguished poets, priests, and artists.   Its name, Kioto, denotes the City of Peace, and its best citizens were thought to be the

IN KIOTO.

most refined and polished of a race whose gentle manners are still unsurpassed.

Our hotel in Kioto was unlike the inns of other Japanese cities, being neither a European structure, like the hotels at Tokio and Yokohama, nor yet a tea-house, such as we had lately seen.   It was a compromise between the two, with comfortable rooms and foreign furnishings.   Its situation is far above the city, upon a wooded hill that has been sacred to Buddha for a thousand years.   Around it are old temples, monasteries, and pagodas, among which one can walk in shaded paths the livelong day.   Often, while seated on the spacious hotel balcony which overlooks the town, we heard a strangely fascinating sound rolling toward us through the sacred groves in solemn, silvery vibrations. We discovered after a short walk the cause of this. It was a huge bronze bell,— no less than seventy-four tons in weight,— whose sweet-voiced call to prayer has echoed over this hill for nearly three hundred years. There are few sounds more pleasing to the ear than the vibrations of a distant, deep-toned bell. Except in Russia I had never heard such notes as those that issue from the bells of old Japan. Their solemn strokes swell through the forest like the crescendo of an orchestra. These bells, however, are not rung, like ours, by wrenching them from side to side, until a pendant tongue falls sharply on their inner rim. Ah, no! the Japanese treat them far more cleverly. Suspended from the belfry roof is a

YAAMI'S HOTEL, KIOTO.

large, rounded shaft of wood. An attendant swings this to one side, and lets it fall, to strike the inverted bowl of bronze one mighty blow. The difference in sound produced by using wood instead of metal, is astonishing. There is no grating jar, no sharpness in the tone, but one stupendous boom of sound, as though a musical cannon were discharged,

A MONSTER BELL, KIOTO.

This instantly re-solves itself into slow-moving, ever widening circles of reverbera-tion, which fall upon the ear more and more faintly, till they die away like the last murmur of the surf upon the sand.

Accepting the in-vitation which that bell conveyed to us, we strolled toward one of Ki-oto's many temples. In the one we entered, five bells, with long white cords attached, were hanging in the lacquered porch. The worshiper pulls one of these, to call the atten-tion of the god; then, having said a prayer, he drops a coin into a grated box and goes his way. On one occasion, we saw a pret-ty baby, three

A TEMPLE IN KIOTO.

BRONZE HORSE.

months old, brought hither in its mother's arms, and made to pull the bell-rope with its tiny hand. Then the great-grand-mother of the child, herself almost eighty-six years old, advanced with trembling limbs and rang it for the second time. It was a suggestive picture,—this vision of old age and infancy, like opposite poles of an electric battery, completing here a circuit of four generations; pathetic emblems of the

A JAPANESE BELFRY.

past and future,—the smiling infant looking forward to anticipated blessings, the feeble matron thankful for the gifts received.

The Japanese have really two religions, in some respects rivals of each other. The elder, or original faith, is Shintoism; the younger, which has struggled to supplant it for twelve hundred years, is Buddhism.

It is difficult to comprehend exactly what Shintoism is. The name means, literally, "The way of the gods," but it is

A SHINTO PRIEST.

the vaguest known religion. It has no bible, no dogmas, and not even a moral code. It dimly hints at immortality, but has no definite heaven or hell. Its gods are either deified national heroes or else personifications of nature, such as the glorious sun, the all-surrounding ocean, and the innumerable deities of mountains, rivers, rocks, and trees. Its shrines for worship, with their gray stone lanterns and majestic *torii*, are severely plain, its services extremely simple, and all its priests appear like laymen in the streets, donning their clerical robes

ENTRANCE TO A JAPANESE TEMPLE.

only when they officiate in the temples.

Not so the Buddhist priests. Their costume, like their ritual, is imposing. While Shinto priests may marry, the Buddhists take the vow of celibacy. In fact, though wholly different in its creed from the great Roman Catholic communion, some of the ceremonials of Buddhism remind us of it; such as their richly-

BUDDHIST PRIESTS.

mantled priests, their altars bright with candles and adorned with flowers, their clouds of incense, grand processionals, and

BUDDHIST PRIESTS IN A CEMETERY.

statues of the gods and saints. What wonder, then, since it has such attractions, that this religion, when it came hither from India, about six centuries after Christ, achieved at once a remarkable success? The colder Shinto faith lost ground,

INTERIOR OF A JAPANESE TEMPLE.

and even the Mikados gave to Buddha's doctrines favor and support for centuries; but Shintoism has now once more become the state religion.

The furnishings of the Buddhist temples in Japan are often marvels of artistic beauty, comprising tables, columns, doors, and even floors, composed of ruby red or jet-black lacquer, which is so thick and smooth as to produce the effect of rosewood or solid ebony. Here, too, are altars loaded down with ornaments of gold and bronze, silken screens inscribed with sacred characters, exquisite bronze lanterns, incense-burners, gilded gongs, tall lotus-flowers with leaves of gold, and beautiful lacquered boxes placed on stands about the floor, within which are the precious manuscripts of

Buddhist scriptures. In a word, recall the richest specimens of Japanese art that you have ever seen, and know that with such adornment the finest temples in Japan are filled.

In some of the less important Buddhist shrines, however, "all that glitters is not gold." Some temples are repulsive from their shabby ornaments, hideous idols, and gaudy paper lanterns. Some of their deities are enthroned behind a wooden grating, and worshipers tie to the latter a bit of cloth on which has been inscribed a petition. One such deity, we were assured, has for his special function the assisting of women to obtain good husbands. He is immensely popular. We saw, in half an hour, at least a dozen women knock on the grating to rouse him and entreat his services. One old woman, who evidently knew from experience how rare good husbands are, led two of her daughters to the gate, and pounded on it savagely three times. Yet even in that temple we found a proof of how the western world has invaded the customs of Japan; for here, amid the grotesque deities, was hung

A BUDDHIST TEMPLE.

an eight-day clock, which proved on examination to have come from Ansonia, Connecticut!

A singular feature of many of these Buddhist temples is a line of votive tablets, erected by pious souls, who wished

either to show by means of pictures the dangers from which
God had rescued them, or else to certify, in written words,
to miraculous answers to their prayers. The Buddhist religion, however, despite its age and its indubitable hold upon
the people, is not to-day, as we have said, the official religion
of Japan. Since 1869 the Government has favored Shintoism, and many Buddhist temples have been stripped of their
magnificent decorations and dedicated to the Shinto faith.

VOTIVE PICTURES.

Accordingly, the
contributions
that once came
freely from the
people are now
falling off, and
it is difficult to
keep in good re-
pair the costly
lacquer work
and gilding of
the temples.
Some shrines
already look
shabby and neg-
lected. How-
ever, an occasional exception to this rule shows how dangerous it is to make unqualified statements about Japan.

    In Kioto, for example, we found a most astonishing proof
of the vitality of Japanese Buddhism in the new and splendid
temple of Higashi Hongwanji, which at the time of our visit
was in process of construction. We saw it on the occasion of
a special festival, when popular recognition and acclaim were
manifested in profuse and elaborate decorations. But, the
truth is, the temple is continually receiving the support of
untold thousands of the Japanese. All the surrounding

A PYRAMID WITH SILVER CREST.

provinces have given it, not only money, but timber, metals, and stone, besides the transportation of materials free of cost. It seems as if conservative and faithful Buddhists, indignant at the prevalent idea that their religion is declining, were making this stupendous effort to show the world their strength and their devotion.

One object in this shrine especially impressed us. This was a pile of rope,—each strand as long and large as a ship's

NEW BUDDHIST TEMPLE IN KIOTO.

cable,—made of women's hair, twisted and spliced with hemp! These ropes are the offerings of poor but devout women, thousands of whom, in nine Japanese provinces, having nothing else to give, contributed their hair, to be woven into cables for hoisting beams and tiles in the construction of the temple. One rope, two hundred and fifty feet in length, was the gift of three thousand five hundred women in one province alone. This seems at first, perhaps, a trifling thing; but when one recollects the pride which Japanese women take in their abundant hair, the care they show in its arrangement, and the entire absence in Japan of hats or bonnets to conceal

the sacrifice, their action is remarkable. And when we perceived among the usual black strands occasional streaks of
white and gray, proving that this enthusiasm extended from
youth to age, it seemed to us the most touching proof of popular devotion to a sacred cause that we had ever seen.

We witnessed a number of *matsuris*, or religious festivals
in Japan, when all the principal streets were thronged with
people, and even the house-tops held their private box-par-

ROPES OF WOMEN'S HAIR.

ties. On every
such occasion
there would ap-
pear, in the cen-
tre of the thor-
oughfare, an ob-
ject that never
failed to fill us
with amazement.
Think of a hun-
dred men pulling
madly on two
ropes, and draw-
ing thus a kind
of car, mounted
on two enormous
wooden wheels.

Resting on this, and rising far above the neighboring roofs,
imagine a portable shrine, resembling a pagoda, with roof of
gold, and gorgeously decorated with silken tapestries, which
are so richly embroidered and heavily gilded as to be valued
at many thousands of dollars. This structure had two stories,
on each of which were many life-size figures,— some being
actual men and women, while others were mere painted
statues, hideous and grotesque. Behind this came another
car, shaped like a huge bird with crested head. Upon this

second vehicle also stood an edifice, three stories high, resplendent with magnificent tapestries and gilded ornaments, and bearing statues of old Japanese deities, so laughably grotesque, that had not their surroundings been

A RELIGIOUS FESTIVAL.

so rich the whole procession would have seemed a farce. Some of these statues, which were made to open their mouths

A MATSURI.

and wag their heads like puppets, were especially applauded. Men, women, and children rode upon these cars, blowing horns and beating drums. If we had closed our eyes, we might have thought that we were listening to a

Fourth of July parade of the "Antiques and Horribles." What most impressed us was the absence of what we should consider religious feeling. It was a show, a brilliant pageant—nothing more; though, as such, it was heartily enjoyed by thousands.

A CHARACTERISTIC STREET.

The streets in Kioto, like those of most Japanese cities, are usually much alike. No heavy teams disturb their rounded surfaces. Few vehicles, save light jinrikishas, pass over them. Almost no animals are ever seen in them. They are as clean as sidewalks are with us. In most of them we can perceive some groups or individuals, arrayed in varied colors, moving about like brilliant fragments in a long kaleidoscope. On either side extends a line of little houses, which, in point of architectural effect, appear monotonous, but since their lower stories are all open to the street, and from the fact that most of them are shops with all their goods on exhibition two feet from the thoroughfare, they really offer infinite variety.

Approaching one of these shops, one first encounters a wooden platform, two feet from the ground. On this the

Japanese purchaser usually seats himself, as he prepares to
bargain. Most foreigners, however, being unable to fold
comfortably their limbs beneath them for a cushion, assume a
different attitude, and allow their feet to hang over the side.
If they ascend the platform and really enter the shop, they
are supposed to leave their shoes below, and walk in stocking
feet; for the shops of the Japanese are, like their houses,
paved with polished wood or covered with spotless matting.
The goods displayed by no means constitute the merchant's
entire stock. The choicest articles are often in a fire-proof
store-house, close at hand, and can be sent for at a moment's
notice. As for the contents of these street bazaars, they

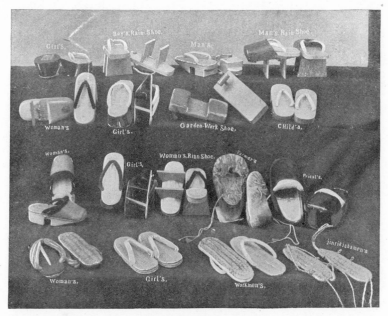

STYLES OF JAPANESE SANDALS.

comprise every article of clothing, ornament, and furniture
conceivable by the Japanese mind.

The shoe shops in particular were, at first, a source of
great surprise to us. "These surely are not shoes," we said,

92 JAPAN

SHOPPING MADE EASY.

as we beheld their great variety of foot-coverings. And yet the Japanese are shod, though sandals is a better name than shoes, for what they wear. A Japanese gentleman, who has not yet adopted European dress, wears in the house a cotton sock, which has a separate compartment for the great toe, like the thumb of a mitten. When he walks out, he plants his foot on a straw sandal, or, if the streets be muddy, on a wooden clog that rises three inches from the ground. In doing so, he thrusts the apex of a V-shaped cord between his great toe and the smaller ones, and, holding on his sandals thus, he marches off.

But not all the merchants of Kioto are content to stay in shops; and, in this respect, human nature is much the same the world over. The gorgeous vehicles

A FLOWER MERCHANT.

JAPANESE HANDIWORK.

of American country peddlers, which we admired in our childhood days, are reproduced here on a smaller scale, though
without wheels; and as the Japanese are sure to be artistic in
everything, we were not surprised to find their brooms and
dusters grouped in clusters like a huge bouquet.   The peddlers themselves are pictures of human placidity.   It is true,
their eyes will open somewhat at the sight of foreigners, but
most of the beardless faces that one sees beneath their mush-
room hats of straw might easily serve an artist as models
for a Japanese
grandmother.

In strolling
through the
streets, we often
paused to watch
the natives at
their work.   If,
for example, it
chanced to be a
cobbler making
wooden clogs,
we saw, to our
astonishment,
that his great

MAKING CLOGS.

toe could hold a block of wood as firmly as a thumb, and we
began to ask ourselves if western workmen had gained much
by covering up the feet and losing a third hand.   The methods of Japanese laborers seem to us, at first, a little clumsy,
because they are unlike our own.   But one soon comes to
marvel at their skill.   No nation is superior to them in dex-
terity, fineness of touch, and delicacy of finish.   In great
things, as in small, one finds the same perfection.   Japanese carpenters, for example, will use few nails in building a
house, but they will make mortises so exact that water cannot

CHILD AND NURSE.

penetrate between the joints; and they will decorate a fan or paint a photographic slide with touches so delicate that they will bear inspection with a magnifying-glass. To watch them is like watching our own motions in a mirror, for everything appears reversed. Our carpenters push the plane from them; the Japanese pull it toward them. The threads of our screws turn to the right; theirs turn to the left. Our keys turn outward; theirs turn inward. Nor is this difference true of handicraft alone. Their way of doing hundreds of familiar things is so directly opposite to ours, that one is almost tempted to believe the cause to be their relative position on the other side of the globe, and that they are really living upside down. The only question is: "Which side is up, and which is down?" The Japanese think our ways just as strange as we do theirs. We, for example, carry our babies in our arms; in Japan, however, they are strapped on the backs of children not much larger than themselves, their little heads being

JAPANESE CARPENTERS.

left to flop about like flowers half-broken from the stem. Nor
is this custom the exception. It is the universal rule, alike in
city streets and country lanes. Whole pages could be filled
in mentioning points of difference between Japanese and
European customs. Thus, we stand erect before distinguished men, in token of respect; the Japanese, on the contrary, sit down. We take off our hats when we enter a
house, while they remove their shoes. Our books begin at
the left; theirs
at the right; and
if they have any
"foot-notes,"
they are placed
at the top of the
page. We write
across a sheet of
paper horizon-
tally; they write
vertically down
the page, like
we make a col-
umn of figures.
Our color for
mourning is
black; theirs is

MAT-MAKERS.

white. The best rooms in our houses are in front; theirs are
in the rear. We mount our horses from the left; they from
the right. We put a horse head foremost into a stall; they
back him in and fasten him in the front. On seeing this, we
laughingly recalled the showman's trick of getting people to
"come and see a horse's head where his tail should be."

But if the Japanese are proficient in the ordinary industries of life, what shall be said of those finer proofs of their
artistic skill which charm the world? At first, the foreigner
hardly comprehends the value of their work or the amount of

CLOISONNÉ VASES.

time and labor it has cost. Their articles of *cloisonné* are unsurpassed. In everything relating to handicraft in bronze the Japanese are unexcelled. Their flowered lacquer-work, also, with figures raised in gold, has been perfected for a thousand years; while in the realm of silk embroidery and gold brocade the Japanese have been said to paint with the needle as other artists do with the brush. In brief, they have produced among themselves and for themselves, for centuries, unnumbered masterpieces of artistic excellence, and this without a particle of outside help save that which came to them originally from China. Not, therefore, as uncultured mendicants have they appeared upon the threshold of the western world; but rather

ONE OF JAPAN'S HUGE BELLS.

as people who, while accepting much that we have gained, have also not a little of value to impart.   Hence they are a nation that elicits, not merely interest and astonishment, but also admiration and respect.

There is a fascination in watching a Japanese artist engaged in *cloisonné* work.   Taking a copper vase, he traces on its surface certain figures, such as flowers, birds, and trees. Then, from a roll of brass, one-sixteenth of an inch in

" IN THE GLOAMING."

breadth, he cuts off tiny pieces which, with consummate skill, and by eye-measurement alone, he twists into a mass of lines which correspond exactly to the figures he has drawn.   Holding these bits of brass between the points of tweezers, he touches them with glue, and deftly locates them upon the rounded surface of the vase.   At length, when all the figures are outlined, as it were, in skeleton, the flesh has to be applied.   In other words, the thousands of interstices between the lines of brass are filled up with enamel of all shades and colors.   When this is done the jar is put into a furnace, then

A SERENADE.

touched with
more enamel,
then fired again,
and so on, till it
has been brought
to the required
degree of artistic
finish. Then it
is polished with
great care, until
the shining edges
of the brass
show through
the enamel like
the veins of a leaf.   The colors also, by this time, are perfectly
distinct and permanent, and the entire work stands forth,— a
marvelous combination of delicacy, strength, and beauty.

The scene, at evening, on the river-bank at Kioto is charming. Along the
water's edge are
numerous little
tea-houses, in
front of which
are many wood-
en piers. These
are divided
off into little
squares, like
private boxes
in a theatre, and
in them groups
of Japanese are
seated,— smok-
ing, or taking

A WAYSIDE MONUMENT.

supper in the open air. Meantime, a thousand colored lanterns gleam like fireflies on either shore and fleck the river
with a dust of gold.

One cannot, however, praise the music which is here produced. It would be highly amusing, if one were deaf; but
when one's hearing is acute, a little of such music goes a long
way. None of the most enthusiastic admirers of the Japanese has dared, as yet, to praise their music. To Occidental ears the twanging of their banjo strings, and, above

PRIESTLY MUSICIANS.

all, their caterwaulings, are positive torture. And yet, it must
be said that to the Japanese our music seemed at first no less
absurd than theirs to us. At the first opera given in Tokio
by a European company, the Japanese audience was con-
vulsed with laughter, and when the prima donna sang her
highest notes, some men and women could no longer control
themselves, and were seen stuffing their handkerchiefs into
their mouths to avoid uttering shrieks of merriment.

In the immediate vicinity of Kioto is a bamboo grove
possessing an extent and beauty unusual even in Japan,
where the plant grows luxuriantly. The various ways in

which the Japanese use the bamboo stalk afforded us con-
tinual amusement and surprise, while it challenged admiration
for their ingenuity.   Bridges and scaffolding supports, water-
pipes and fences, furniture, umbrellas, baskets, fans, hats,
pipe-stems, sandals, screens, and walking-sticks,—are all con-

BAMBOO GROVE NEAR KIOTO.

structed from that jointed, hollow stem, which looks so light
and delicate, yet in reality is strong and durable.   A thing
of beauty and utility, the bamboo is certainly one of the
greatest blessings that Nature has bestowed upon her children
in the Land of the Rising Sun.

A pretty sight in traveling through the province of Uji,
near Kioto, are its tea-plantations, consisting of acres of

evergreen bushes, two or three feet high. Among these move and sparkle in the sun odd bits of color, which prove to be the scanty robes of women and children crouching among the plants and picking their leaves. Most of these tea-plants are left unsheltered from the sun and storm, but the more valuable shrubs, producing tea worth six or seven dollars a pound, are covered by a trellis of bamboo, on which straw mats are placed. Sometimes the floor of an entire valley will be concealed beneath these mattings, which resemble a gigantic tent. It is a curious fact that, unlike teas from India and China, Japanese tea must not be made with boiling water, as that gives it a bitter flavor. Indeed, the finer the quality of the

A TEA-PLANTATION.

tea the cooler must be the water. Tea is the national beverage of Japan, and has been largely used there for nearly a thousand years. The Japanese hotels are known as "teahouses," which correspond also to the *cafés* of Europe. The *cha-no-yu*, or fashionable ceremony of serving and drinking tea, has been for seven hundred years a national institution, governed by the minutest etiquette, each action and each gesture being regulated by a code of rules. It is said to have originated in a formal style of tea-drinking among the Buddhist priests, who found the beverage an easy means of keeping themselves awake during their nocturnal vigils. Japan may be said, therefore, not only to owe the introduction of the tea-plant to a celebrated Buddhist saint, who imported it from China, but for her elaborate ceremony of tea-drinking to be still further indebted to the priests of Buddhism.

While walking one day in Kioto, we met a fellow-passenger from Vancouver.

TEA-PICKERS.

" What places have you visited?" he asked.

We told him.

" Have you not been to Haruna, beyond Ikao?" he inquired.

" No," we replied. " We thought of going there, but finally decided to omit it."

" You made a great mistake!" he cried. " Why not retrace your steps and go there now?   It is not too late."

" That means," we said, " in all, six hundred miles of extra travel."

"No mat-
ter," he insist-
ed. "You had
better do it."

"Are you
quite serious?"

"Not only
serious, but en-
thusiastic. You
will never regret
it. Go!"

We followed
his advice, and
a few days later,
one afternoon
in late October,

SACRED ROCKS AND TREES.

we found ourselves almost the only guests in a well-kept tea-
house in Ikao. Swift 'rikisha men had brought us hither
from the railway station, sixteen miles away. The air was
most exhilarating, for we were three thousand feet above the

IKAO.

sea, which we
had left eight
hours before
at Yokohama.
Around us on
all sides were
lofty moun-
tains, whose
hidden treas-
ures could not
be explored in
jinrikishas, for
this was another
point where all

roads terminate, and only paths lead inward to the fabled
homes of mountain deities.

It was four o'clock the next morning when we started.
It was still dark. The stars were glorious. We knew the
coming day would be superb. It was as yet too cold for riding, so, followed by our kago-bearers, we set forth on foot.
For some time we walked on in silence, enraptured with the

THE PATH THROUGH THE FOREST.

splendor of the sky. Above us gleamed the Dipper's seven
diamond points; Orion's belt hung radiant amid a galaxy of
other suns; while, just above a lofty mountain range, flashed
with unwonted brilliancy the herald of approaching day. At
length the stellar light began to pale. The east became first
white, then golden, as the sun advanced, and then there
came an hour's scenery that can never be effaced from my
memory.

LAKE BIWA.

The colors on the mountains were magnificent. Autumnal foliage mantled them with glory. Thousands of oaks and maples lined the slopes with every shade of orange, red, vermilion, green, and purple. In any light these varied tints would have been beautiful; but to behold them changing into glory, tree by tree, as the first touch of dawn awakened them from sleep, was such a vision as we had never hoped to look upon. Some of this radiant foliage bedecked the ground, and sometimes we

walked ankle-deep through multicolored leaves.

THE STAIRCASE AT HARUNA.

Moreover, the pathway was all white with frost, and stretched away in glittering perspective through the trees, like an avenue of silver between mountains of jewels. Intoxicated with such sights and with the crisp, aromatic air of that October dawn, we walked for miles without fatigue, unable to repress at times our exclamations of enthusiasm.

After a time, we found ourselves at the entrance to a deep ravine, shaded by giant trees, which at that early hour were still unburnished by the sun. In view of the reverence felt by the Japanese for massive rocks and time-gnarled trees, it is not strange that this wild gorge of Haruna has been for ages looked upon as sacred. A feeling of solemnity stole over us. Instinctively we spoke in softer tones. I felt as once before, when sailing into a Norwegian fjord. It was a place for Dante to describe and for Doré to illustrate.

At length we saw, wedged in between two mighty rocks, a flight of stone steps leading to a lacquered gate. Our Japanese attendant immediately bowed his head, removed his sandals, and knelt down to pray. Nor was this strange. Who could resist, in such a place, the impulse to revere that Power of which these forms of nature were imperfect symbols? At all events, whatever may have been the difference in our creeds, both traveler and native worshiped here that day,—one standing in the forest shade, the other kneeling on the moss-grown steps.

After some moments' silence, our attendant arose and began the ascent. We followed him. On passing the first

"HUGE CRYPTOMERIAS
LIKE THOSE OF NIKKO."

gateway, we perceived another smaller portal, which seemed to lead directly into the cliff. Above it was a rock, a hundred and fifty feet in height, and shaped like a gigantic obelisk. Around it rose huge cryptomerias, like

THE HEART OF OLD JAPAN.

those of Nikko, wrinkled with age, and solemn in their sanctity and shade. The mountain-side so overhung the place

SACRED PORTAL.

that it seemed kept from falling only by a caprice of nature. We almost feared to speak, lest, like some Alpine avalanche, the monstrous mass might fall and overwhelm us. Finally, however, we passed beneath the second arch; and, lo! before us, on a shelf of rock, completely isolated from the outer world, and guarded by these sentinels of stone, we saw a sacred shrine.   Even at that early hour one pilgrim was already here, and, as the radiance of the rising sun stole through the twilight of the holy grove and turned the temple steps to gold, unconscious of the picture he produced, he knelt in prayer.

That scene can never be forgotten.   An interval of centuries seemed to separate us from the Japan of Yokohama. No whisper of approaching change had yet penetrated these peaceful solitudes.   No earthquake shock of doubt had sent a tremor through this mountain altar.   The faith which chose this immemorial forest for its temple still reigned here supreme. And as we stood by this illumined portico, in which a ray of sunlight glittered like a sacred fire, we felt that we had reached the Heart of Old Japan.

CHINA

CHINA

CHINA defies the world to equal her in three important respects: age, population, and industries. As for the first, she undoubtedly has the oldest Government on earth. Even the Papacy is young compared with it; and as for our republic, it is a thing of yesterday. A Chinaman once said to an American: "Wait till your Government has been tried before you boast of it. What is a hundred years? Ours has stood the test of forty centuries. When you did not exist, we were. When you shall have passed away, we still shall be."

In point of numbers, too, the Chinese empire leads the world. Its area is nearly twice as large as that of the United States, and it has six times as many people. The governor of one Chinese province rules over sixty million souls. Have we a definite conception of what four hundred million human beings are? Arrange the inhabitants of our globe in one long line, and every fourth man will be a Chinaman.

EMPEROR OF CHINA.

As for her industries, Musa, the Saracen conqueror of Spain, once aptly said that Wisdom, when she came from heaven to earth, was lodged in the head of the Greeks, the tongue of the Arabs, and the hands of the Chinese. China

was once what the United States is now—the birthplace of
inventions.   Paper was manufactured there in the third century of our era.   Tea was produced a century later.   If
Europe had enjoyed communication with China, it would

A CHINESE TEMPLE.

have learned the art of printing many centuries before it did;
and who can say what might have been the result?   A thousand years ago the Chinese made designs on wood.   Printing from stone was a still earlier industry among them.   In
China, also, gunpowder was first invented—a thought by
which, alas! so many thoughts have been destroyed.   This
same astonishing race produced the mariner's compass in the
fourth century, porcelain in the third, chess and playing-
cards in the twelfth, and silk embroideries in almost prehis-
toric times.   An empire, therefore, of such vast antiquity,

overwhelming population, and great achievements must be, despite its faults, a country of absorbing interest.

The most delightful portion of the voyage from Japan to China lies in the Japanese Mediterranean, known as the Inland Sea. It is a miniature ocean, practically land-locked for three hundred miles, with both shores constantly in sight, yet strewn with islands of all shapes and sizes, from small and uninhabited rocks to wave-encircled hills, terraced and culti-vated to their very summits. It seems as if volcanic action here had caused the land to sink, until the ocean rushed in and submerged it, leaving only the highest peaks above the waves.

We lingered here all day upon the steamer's deck, like passengers on the Rhine, fearing to lose a single feature of the varied panorama gliding by on either side. By night it was more glorious even than by day; for then, from every danger-

THE JAPANESE MEDITERRANEAN.

ous cliff flashed forth a beacon light; the villages along the shore displayed a line of glittering points, like constellations rising from the sea; and, best of all, at a later hour, moon-light lent enchantment to the scene, drawing a crystal edge

WAVE-ENCIRCLED HILLS.

along each mountain crest, and making every island seem a
jewel on a silver thread.

When we emerged from these inland waters, we saw between us and the setting sun the stretch of ocean called the
China Sea.   At certain seasons of the year this is the favorite
pathway of typhoons; and the Formosa Channel, in particular, has been   a graveyard for countless vessels. Indeed,   only three weeks before, a sister

HUGE SAILS LIKE THE WINGS OF BATS.

ship of ours—the "Bokhara,"—had gone down here in a terrific cyclone. Yet when we sailed its waters nothing could have been more beautiful. Day after day this sea of evil omen rested motionless, like a sleek tigress gorged with food and basking in the sun.

After a three-days' voyage from the Japanese coast, we began to meet, in constantly increasing numbers, large, pointed boats, propelled by huge sails ribbed with cross-bars, like the wings of bats. Upon the bow of each was painted an

THE HARBOR OF HONG-KONG.

enormous eye; for of their sailing craft the mariners of China, in elementary English, say: "If boat no have eye, how can boat see go?" We were assured that these were Chinese sailing craft, and that our destination was not far away; but it was difficult to realize this, and I remember looking off beyond those ships and trying to convince myself that we were actually on the opposite side of the globe from home and friends, and in a few brief hours were to land in that vast Eastern empire so full of mystery in its exclusiveness, antiquity, and changeless calm.

That night the agitation that precedes one's first arrival in a foreign land made sleep almost impossible. It seemed to me that I had not closed my eyes when suddenly the steamer stopped. To my astonishment, the morning light had already found its way into my state-room. We had arrived! Hurrying to the deck, therefore, I looked upon the glorious harbor of Hong-Kong. A hundred ships and steamers lay at anchor here, displaying flags of every country on the globe. Although the day had hardly dawned, these waters

THE CITY OF VICTORIA.

showed great animation. Steam-launches, covered with white awnings, were darting to and fro like flying-fish. Innumerable smaller boats, called *sampans*, propelled by Chinese men and women, surrounded each incoming steamer, like porpoises around a whale. On one side rose some barren-looking mountains, which were a part of the mainland of China; but for the moment they presented little to attract us. It was the other shore of this magnificent harbor that awoke our interest; for there we saw an island twenty-seven miles in circumference, covered with mountains rising boldly from the sea.

THE PUBLIC GARDENS.

Along the base of one of these elevations, and built in terraces far up on its precipitous slopes, was a handsome city.

"What is this?" we inquired eagerly.

"The town itself," was the reply, "is called Victoria, but this imposing island to whose flank it clings, is, as you may suppose, Hong-Kong."

The first impression made upon me here was that of mild astonishment at the architecture. Almost without exception, the prominent buildings of Victoria have on every story deep porticoes divided by columns into large, square spaces, which

A STREET IN HONG-KONG.

from a distance look like letter-boxes in a post-office. We soon discovered that such deep, shadowy verandas are essential here, for as late as November it was imprudent not to carry a white umbrella, and even before our boat had brought us from the steamer to the pier, we perceived that the solar rays were not to be trifled with.

As soon as possible after landing, we started to explore this British settlement. I was delighted with its streets and buildings. The former are broad, smooth and clean; the latter, three or four stories high, are built of granite, and even on a curve have sidewalks shielded from the sun or rain by

the projection of the roof above. Truly, the touch of England has wrought astounding changes in the fifty-five years
that she has held this island as her own. Before she came
it was the resort of poverty-stricken fishermen and pirates.

DEEP PORTICOES AND COLONNADES.

But now the city of Victoria alone contains two hundred
thousand souls, while the grand aqueducts and roads which
cross the mountains of Hong-Kong are worthy to be compared with some of the monumental works of ancient Rome.
    Along the principal thoroughfare in Victoria, the banks,
shops, hotels, and club-houses, which succeed each other rapidly, are built of the fine gray granite of the adjacent mountains, and show handsome architectural designs. Everything
looks as trim and spotless as the appointments of a man-of-
war. Even the district of the town inhabited by Chinamen
is kept by constant watchfulness immeasurably cleaner than
a Chinese city; although if one desires to see the world-wide
difference that exists between the British and Mongolian races,

he merely needs to take a short walk through the Chinese quarter of Victoria. But such comparisons may well be deferred until one reaches Canton. There one beholds the genuine native article.

The police who guard the lives and property of the residents of Hong-Kong, are for the most part picked men of English birth, and are considered as trustworthy as regular troops. But several hundred of these guardians of the peace are Sikhs—a race imported hither from India—renowned for bravery, loyal to the British government, and having no sympathy with the Chinese. These Sikhs have handsome faces, brilliant eyes, and dark complexions, the effect of which is wonderfully en-   hanced by their immense red   turbans, con-

THE BANK, HONG-KONG.

spicuous two or three blocks away, not only by their startling color, but because their wearers exceed in stature all other races in Hong-Kong.

Strolling one morning through the outskirts of the city, I came upon some troops engaged in military manœuvres, and

attired in white from head to foot, to shield them from the
sun. What traveler in the East can forget the ever-present
soldiers of Great Britain, of whom there are nearly three

POLICEMEN.

thousand in
the garrison of
Hong-Kong? I
know it is fre-
quently the
fashion to sneer
at them and to
question their
efficiency in
case of war. I
know, too, that
in certain ways the vast extent of England's empire constitutes
her weakness. But I must say that in a tour around our planet
I was impressed as never before with what the British had accomplished in the way of conquest, and with the number of
strategic points they hold in every quarter of the globe. We
had but recently left the western terminus of England's North

American pos-
sessions, yet in
a few days we
discerned the
flag of England
flying at Hong-
Kong. Next
we beheld the
Union Jack at
Singapore, then
at Penang, then

SOLDIERS DRILLING.

at Ceylon, and after that throughout the length and breadth
of the vast empire of India, as well as the enormous area
of Burma. Leaving Rangoon, if we sail southward, we are

CHINESE COBBLER.

reminded that the southernmost portion of Africa is entirely
in English hands, as well as the huge continent of Australia.
Returning northward, we find the same great colonizing power
stationed at the   mouth of the
Red Sea, in   the British

citadel of   Aden.   Again
a trifling journey,   and we reach
Egypt, *via* the Suez   Canal, both vir-

tually controlled to-   day by England. Then, like the three stars in Orion's belt, across the
Mediterranean lie Cyprus, Malta, and Gibraltar; in fact, we
find one mighty girdle of imposing strongholds all the way,
bristling with cannon, guarded by leviathans in armor, and

garrisoned by thousands of such soldiers as were drilling at Hong-Kong.

One of the first desires of the visitor to Hong-Kong is to explore the mountain which towers above the city of Victoria to a height of nearly two thousand feet. To do this with the least exertion, each of our party took a canvas-covered bamboo chair, supported by long poles, which Chinese coolies carry on their shoulders. On level ground, two of these bearers were enough, but on the mountain roads three or

CHAIR-COOLIES AT HONG-KONG.

four men were usually needed. To my surprise, I found the motion of these chairs agreeable. The poles possess such elasticity that, leaning back, I was rocked lightly up and down without the least unpleasant jar. In fact, at times the rhythm of that oscillation gave me a sense of drowsiness difficult to resist.

But, alas! we had not here for carriers the cleanly natives of Japan. It may be, as some residents of Hong-Kong assert, that Chinamen are more trustworthy and honest than the Japanese, but certainly in point of personal attractiveness the contrast between these races is remarkable. The bodies of the lower classes of Chinese reveal no evidence of that care so characteristic of the natives of Japan. Their teeth are often yellow tusks; their nails resemble eagle's claws; and their unbecoming clothes seem glazed by perspiration. Nor is there usually anything in their manner to redeem all this. Where the light-hearted Japs enjoy their work, and laugh and talk, the Chinese coolies labor painfully, and rarely smile,

THE MOUNTAIN ABOVE VICTORIA.

regarding you meantime with a supercilious air, as if despising you for being what they call "a foreign devil."

Nevertheless, despite the repulsive appearance of our bearers, we thoroughly enjoyed our excursion up the mountain. At every step our admiration was increased for the magnificent roads which wind about the cliffs in massive terraces, arched over by majestic trees, bordered by parapets of stone, lighted with gas, and lined with broad, deep aqueducts, through which at times the copious rainfall rushes like a mountain stream. It will be seen that such a comparison is not an exaggeration, when I add that not many years ago, thirty-two inches of rain fell here in thirty hours. This mountain is the favorite abode of wealthy foreigners, and hence these curving avenues present on either side, almost to

THE CABLE-ROAD TO VICTORIA PEAK.

the summit, a series of attractive villas commanding lovely views. On account of their situation, the gardens of these hillside homes are necessarily small; but in the midst of them, about five hundred feet above the town, a charming botanical park has been laid out.

Forgetful of our coolies at the gate, we lingered in this garden for an hour or two, delighted with its fine display of semitropical foliage.   It is marvelous what skillful gardeners have accomplished here, in transforming what was fifty years ago a barren rock into an open-air conservatory.   Palms, banyans, india-rubber trees, mimosas with their tufts of gold, camellias with their snowy blossoms—all these are here, with

roses, mignonette, and jessamine, surrounded with innumerable ferns.   Occasionally we encountered in this fragrant area
a Chinese gentleman, indulging leisurely his love of flowers;
for this delightful park is open to all without regard to race
or creed, although the population of the island is extremely
cosmopolitan.   Englishmen, Americans, Germans, French-
men, Spaniards, Portuguese, Italians, Parsees, Mohamme-
dans, Jews, Hindus, and fully one hundred and fifty thousand
Chinamen, are residents of the city of Victoria alone.

In this retired park one does not realize that Hong-Kong
is such a rendezvous for different nationalities; but frequently,
while we were walking here, the sharp report of a cannon
forced a discordant echo from the neighboring hills and told
us that some foreign man-of-war had just appeared within the

bay ; for here
some ship or
steamer is con-
tinually arriv-
ing or depart-
ing, and many
times a day
there comes a
deafening inter-
change of sa-
lutes that sends
a thrill through
every window-
pane upon the
mountain.

One can well
understand,

THE BOTANICAL PARK, HONG-KONG.

therefore, that with so mixed a population and in such close
proximity to China, the officers sent out here by the British
government must be men of courage, the garrison of the island

strong, and its administration prompt and resolute. A single
incident revealed to me the crimes which would undoubtedly
creep forth, like vipers from a loathsome cave, were they
not kept in check by vigorous justice and incessant vigilance.

In one of the residences on the height above Victoria, I
met one day at dinner the captain of a steamer anchored in
the bay. He asked me to come out some evening and pay a

AN OPEN-AIR CONSERVATORY.

visit to his ship. The following night, soon after dark, I
walked down to the pier, intending to embark on one of the
many boats along the shore. I was about to enter one, when
a policeman rapidly approached. "Give me your name and
number," he said roughly to the Chinese boatman. Then
turning to me, he politely asked my name, address, and destination, and when I intended to return. "I am obliged to
do this," he explained, "for your protection. There is a
population of twenty thousand Chinese living in this harbor

A HONG-KONG STREET—IN THE CHINESE QUARTER.

IN THE BUSINESS SECTION, HONG-KONG.

upon boats alone, besides the usual criminals who drift to
such a place. Before we adopted this precaution, a foreigner
would sometimes embark on one of these craft and never be
seen again. In such a case search was useless. He had disappeared as quietly and thoroughly as a piece of silver
dropped into the bay.''

When I stood on the apex of Victoria Peak, I thought that
I had never seen a finer pros-
pect. Nearly two thou-

VIEW FROM
VICTORIA PEAK.

sand feet below us lay the renowned metropolis of the East
which bears the name of England's queen. From this great
elevation, its miles of granite blocks resembled a stupendous
landslide, which, sweeping downward from this rocky height,
had forced its cracked and creviced mass far out into the bay.
Between this and the mainland opposite, curved a portion of
that ocean-girdle which surrounds the island, and on its surface countless boats and steamers seemed, in the long perspective, like ornaments of bead-work on a lady's belt.

Around the summit of the mountain are several handsome
villas and hotels, whither the residents of Victoria come in
summer to escape the heat; but, as a rule, in riding over the
island I saw outside of the city very few houses, and little
agriculture. The soil of
Hong-Kong is not fer-
tile; but politically and
commercially the island
is immensely valuable, for
England has now made
of it the great emporium
of the Far East, and, garrisoned by British troops,
it guards completely the
approaches to that river,
upon which, ninety-two
miles inland from the
ocean, lies the city of
Canton.

THE RACE-TRACK, HONG-KONG.

One of the pleasantest
excursions in Hong-Kong
may be made in sedan-chairs, some six miles over the hills, to
the great reservoir which supplies the city with water. The
aqueduct which comes from it is solidly constructed, and on its
summit is a granite path protected by iron railings. This

winds along the cliffs for miles, and is in many places cut
through solid rock.   It is an illustration of the handsome, yet
substantial character of everything accomplished here.   One
feels that such works are not only artistic, but enduring.   Here

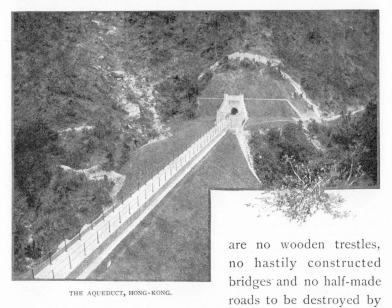

THE AQUEDUCT, HONG-KONG.

are no wooden trestles,
no hastily constructed
bridges and no half-made
roads to be destroyed by
mountain torrents, but everywhere the best of masonry, cyclo-
pean in massiveness and perfect in detail.

On reaching the terminus of this granite pathway we saw
before us the principal reservoir of Hong-Kong.   Though
largely artificial, it looks precisely like a natural lake hidden
away among the mountains.   Before it was constructed the
island's water-supply was lamentably insufficient, and the no-
torious "Hong-Kong fever" gave the place an evil name.
But now, in spite of its large native population, Victoria has
as low a death-rate as most European cities.   The foreign
residents are very proud of these magnificent water-works;
yet, after ten days' sojourn here, when I took leave of several gentlemen by whom I had been entertained in private

houses and at clubs, candor compelled me to confess that, so far as I had been able to observe, the foreign population makes very little use of this water for drinking purposes.

A MOUNTAIN ROAD, HONG-KONG.

On starting to descend the mountain, we found a shorter route than the circuitous path by which we had come — an admirably managed cable-road. In viewing this, the question naturally arises how the Chinese can look on such conveniences as England has here introduced, and still remain content to have in their enormous empire scarcely a decent road, and only a few miles of railway, built to transport coal. Canals

AN EASY DESCENT.

A CHINESE ROAD.

and rivers are still the usual arteries of travel through the most of China. In the northern provinces, where carts are used, the roads are often worn below the surface of the adjacent land, and hence become, in the rainy season, mere water-courses. Travelers are occasionally obliged to swim across them; and cases have been known of people drowning in a Chinese roadway. Moreover, the characteristic carts of China are of the most primitive description, having no seats except the floor, and no springs save the involuntary ones contributed by their luckless passengers. Yet, in many districts, even such vehicles can find no path, and people travel about in wheelbarrows propelled by coolies

A CHINESE VEHICLE.

who are sometimes aided by a sail. The Bishop of North
China, for example, makes many of his parochial visits in
a wheelbarrow.

There is now in China a small progressive party which
favors building railroads, as the Japanese have done, but the
immense majority are against it. Some years ago a foreign
company built a railroad near Shanghai, but the Chinese
speedily bought it up at a great cost, transported the rails and

CHINESE GRAVES.

locomotives to the sea, and left them to rust upon the beach.
This opposition to railways is principally due to the belief
that the use of them would deprive millions of people of their
means of gaining a livelihood, and that they would, moreover, disturb the graveyards of the country. This latter objec-
tion seems at first incredible; but it must be remembered
that Chinese cemeteries are strewn broadcast over the land,

"Thick as autumnal leaves that strow the brooks
In Vallombrosa."

One sees them everywhere, usurping valuable tracts of territory needed for the living. Outside the city of Canton, for

HONG-KONG.

example, there
is a graveyard
thirty miles in
length, in which
are buried fully
one hundred
generations.
Yet the Chinese
insist that not
one grave shall
be disturbed, lest
multitudes of
avenging ghosts

AN ELABORATE TOMB.

should be let loose upon them for such sacrilege.   In fact,
the permanence and inviolability of graves lie at the very
foundation of Chinese life and customs, which is ancestor-
worship.   From childhood to old age the principal duty
of all Chinamen is to propitiate the spirits of their ances-

THE FOREIGN CEMETERY, HONG-KONG.

A FELLOW PASSENGER.

tors, and to make offerings to them regularly at their tombs. This custom cripples the colossal empire of China as paralysis would a giant, and fear of doing violence to their dead holds China's millions in an iron grasp.

The discussion of this theme, as we were descending the mountain, suggested to us the idea of visiting the foreign cemetery in Hong-Kong. In this, as in the public garden, charming results have been obtained by care and irrigation. We were accompanied by a gentleman who had resided on the island nearly thirty years. "In spite of the beauty of this place," he said, "I dread to think that I shall probably be buried here—unable to escape from China even after death. For notwithstanding many pleasant friends, my life, like that of many here, has been at best a dreary banishment from all that makes your Occidental life so stimulating to the intellect

ON THE CANTON RIVER.

and so rich in pleasures. The world at home," he added, "sometimes blames us for faults, the cause of which is often only an intense desire to counteract the loneliness of our existence; and foreigners in the East deserve some sympathy, if only from the fact that in these cemeteries, kept with so much care, the graves of those we love increase so rapidly."

After a few days at Hong-Kong we embarked on one of the American steamers which ply between Victoria and Canton. These boats are modest imitations of the Fall River steamers on Long Island Sound. We found the one that we

RIVER BOATS.

took clean and comfortable and its American captain cordial and communicative. During the trip he related to us many incidents of his life in China. This he could easily do, for there were only two other foreign passengers on board, and hence, so long as we remained upon the promenade deck, the spacious vessel seemed to be our private yacht.

On passing, however, to the deck below, we found a number of Chinamen, likewise going to Canton. Most of them were smoking, lying on their backs, their heads supported by a bale of cloth. At first we thought these constituted all the passengers; but presently we learned, to our astonishment, that farther down, packed in the hold like

sardines in a box, and barricaded from us by an iron grating, were more than a thousand Chinese coolies.   A sentry,
heavily armed, stood by the padlocked grating constantly;
while in the wheel-house and saloon were stands of loaded

EXECUTION OF THE PIRATES.

muskets ready for emergencies.   The danger is that Chinese
pirates will come on board in the disguise of coolies, and at a
favorable moment take possession of the ship.   One naturally
thinks this an impossible occurrence; but only a few years
ago this actually took place on one of these boats.   A well-
armed band of desperadoes swarmed up from the hold, shot
down the captain in cold blood, and also some of the passengers who tried to interfere.   Then, taking command of the
ship, they forced the engineer and crew to do their bidding,
steered to a lonely point where their confederates awaited

them, unloaded the valuable cargo into their boats, disabled the engine so that the survivors could not give the alarm, and finally made their escape. Such are the indisputable facts. Yet, sailing up this peaceful river, reclining in our easy chairs, and soothed by the soft, balmy air, the tragedy seemed so incredible that we were obliged to put our hands upon the guns, in order to realize that precautions were still needed.

As an additional proof, the captain showed us a photograph of the sequel to that act of piracy. For, as a matter of course, the British Government demanded satisfaction for this outrage, and in compliance nineteen criminals were beheaded. Whether they were the actual pirates, however, has been doubted. China always has scores of men awaiting execution—a dozen here, a dozen there. What matters it if those who merit death are said to have committed one crime or another? England had no way of identifying them. Accordingly she shut her eyes, accepted what the Chinese said of them, and took it for granted that the decapitated men were the real culprits. At all events, as an eye-witness told us, the deed itself was quickly done. In each case there was

WITH STARING EYES TURNED UPWARD.

only one swing of the executioner's arm, and one flash of the two-edged sword; then, like a row of flowers clipped from their stems, the heads of all the kneeling criminals were lying in the sand, with staring eyes turned up-ward toward the sky.

AN OLD CHINESE FORT, CANTON RIVER.

On leaving this repulsive picture in the captain's cabin, we found that we were approaching the once important settlement of Whampoa. Its glory is gone now,

OPIUM-SMOKING.

but formerly it played a prom-inent part in Eastern politics and commerce; for previous to the Opium War of 1841 and the establishment of the Treaty Ports, this was as far as foreign ships were permitted to come, and Whampoa was then a kind of counter across which Cantonese and Europeans traded. We now began to observe along the shore strange-looking boats protected by a roof and filled with fruits and vegetables for the Canton market. Moreover, on

SINGING GIRLS.

both sides of the river for many miles we looked on countless
little patches of rice, bananas, oranges, and sugar-cane.   At
one point our attention was called to an island on which are
some old fortifications used by China fifty years ago in her
attempt to exclude opium from her territory.   I suppose that
no intelligent student of the subject doubts that the real cause
of the war of 1841 was the attempt of England to force upon
the Chinese a drug which no one dares to sell in London, even
now, unless it bears the label "poison."   In 1840, the Com-
missioner of
Canton thus
addressed the
Queen of Eng-
land:

A CHINESE BRIDGE.

"How can
your country
seek to acquire
wealth by sell-
ing us an article
so injurious to
mankind ?   I
have heard that
you have a gen-
erous heart; you must be willing, therefore, to obey the
motto of Confucius, and refuse to do to others what you
would not have others do to you."

In an address to foreign traders, issued in 1840, the
Chinese also said: "Reflect that if you did not bring opium
here, where could our people obtain it?   Shall, then, our people die, and your lives not be required?   You are destroying
human life for the sake of gain.   You should surrender your
opium out of regard for the natural feelings of mankind.   If
not, it is right for us to drive every ship of your nation from
our shores."

Finding that these appeals were of no avail, the Chinese finally compelled the British merchants in Canton to give up all the opium in their possession. It amounted to twenty-one thousand chests, or about three million pounds. This

THE CURSE OF CHINA.

mass of poison the Chinese threw into the river, chest after chest, much as Americans treated English tea in Boston harbor. As it dissolved, it is said that a large number of fish died. England retaliated by broadsides from her men-of-war, and in 1842, after an unequal struggle, China was forced to pay her victorious enemy twenty-one million dollars —six millions for the opium destroyed, and fifteen millions as a war indemnity, besides giving to England as her property forever, the island of Hong-Kong, and opening five new ports to foreign trade.

About a century ago opium was rarely used in China except as medicine. To-day it enters through the openings made by English cannon, at the rate of six thousand tons a year, and at an annual profit to the Indian treasury of from thirty to forty million dollars. But this is not the worst: the vice of opium-smoking has spread with such rapidity that in one Chinese city alone, where thirty years ago only five opium dens existed, there are now five thousand. In the minds of many Chinamen, therefore, Christianity is principally associated with the gift of opium and its attendant evils. China has now begun to cultivate the poppy for herself, and in some provinces six-tenths of the land is given over to producing opium, to the great detriment of agriculture. For the Chinese argue that if they must have it anyway, they may as well profit by it themselves, and let their own crop vie with that which England sends from India. It should be said that earnest protests have often been made by conscientious Englishmen against this conduct of their Government, but all

A VILLAGE SCENE.

remonstrances have failed to change its policy. Hence, when our British cousins sometimes humorously say that we Americans worship only the almighty dollar, it may be well to ask if any deity under the sun is more devoutly reverenced than the omnipotent pounds, shillings, and pence.

When we had steamed about five hours from Hong-Kong, we came in sight of our first Chinese pagoda. It is a hollow tower of brick about three hundred feet in height, and resembles, on an enormous scale, one of those tapering sticks which jewelers use for sizing rings. At first, I thought that the nine circular terraces which mark its different stories were adorned with flags or tapestry, but closer scrutiny revealed the melancholy fact that weeds and bushes are now growing here. Indeed, like most of the sacred buildings that I saw in China, it looked both dirty and dilapidated.

Soon after leaving this neglected edifice, we found ourselves amid a constantly increasing throng of Chinese boats, and I began to realize that these were specimens of that "floating population" of Canton of which we have all read, but of which nothing but a visit to it can give an adequate idea.

PAGODA, NEAR CANTON RIVER.

Hardly was our steamer anchored in the stream before the city, when hundreds of these boats closed in upon us on all sides, like cakes of floating ice around a vessel in the Arctic sea. Wedging and pushing frantically, the boatmen almost swamped themselves. They fought for places near the ship like men and women in a panic. The din of voices sounded like the barking of five hundred canines at a dog-show; and Chinese gutturals flew through the air like bullets from a *mitrailleuse*. It seemed impossible to disembark in such a mob.

But suddenly I felt a pressure on my arm. I turned and saw apparently three laundrymen from the United States.

A glance assured me they were father and sons. "Good morning, sir," said one of them in excellent English, "do you know Carter Harrison, of Chicago?"

This question, coming in such a place and at such a time,

NEARING CANTON.

rendered me speechless with astonishment.

"He mentioned us in his book, 'A Race with the Sun,'" continued the young Chinaman. "This is my father, the famous guide, Ah Cum. This is my brother, and I am Ah Cum, Jr. The others are engaged for to-morrow, but I can serve you. Will you take me?"

"So you are Ah Cum?" I rejoined; "I have heard much of you. Your reference book must be a valuable autograph album of distinguished travelers. Yes, we will take you; and, first of all, can you get us safely into one of those boats? And if so, who will guarantee that we shall not be murdered?"

"Ah Cum."

Accordingly we "came," and presently found ourselves in a boat. I cannot relate how we got there. I do not know, myself. I think of it now as one recalls the pulling of a tooth when under the influence of laughing-gas. I have a dim remembrance of jumping from one reeling skiff to another, of stumbling over slippery seats, of holding on to Ah Cum, Sr., and being pushed by Ah Cum, Jr., and now and then grabbing frantically at a Chinese queue, as a drowning man catches at a rope. The only reason that I did not fall into the water is that there was not space enough between the boats. At last, however, bruised and breathless, we reached a place of refuge, and watched our boatmen fight their way out through the crowd, until we landed on the neighboring island of Shameen. After the pandemonium around the steamer, this seemed a perfect paradise of beauty and repose. It is about a mile and a quarter in circumference, and is reserved exclusively for foreigners.

CHINESE BOATS, CANTON.

Shaded by drooping banyan trees, stand many handsome houses inhabited by Englishmen, Germans, and Americans whom the necessities of business keep in banishment here. Their social life is said to be very pleasant, and I should think, indeed, that in so small a settlement the members of this little colony (if they did not hate) would love each other cordially. This pretty place, before the capture of Canton, in 1857, was nothing but a hideous mud-bank. But foreigners have transformed it almost as completely as they have Hong-Kong, and have built around it broad

THE FLOATING HOMES OF THOUSANDS, CANTON.

embankments made of solid granite, which form an agreeable promenade.

Unfortunately, however, Shameen boasts of only one hotel, and of this such dismal stories had been told us that we had half made up our minds to eat and sleep on the American steamers, changing from one to another every morning as they

INTERIOR OF A EUROPEAN'S HOUSE.

came and went. This seemed, however, so difficult, that we resolved to try the accommodations here. We did so, and discovered that in this case "the devil is not so black as he is painted." At all events, clean, comfortable rooms made some amends for a meager bill of fare.

I cherish no delightful recollections of our meals on the island of Shameen. In fact, when a "globe-trotter" has reached India or China, the time has come for him to eat

what he can get, and be devoutly thankful that he can get
anything. Misguided souls who live to eat should never
make a journey around the world. Of course, the foreign
residents here live better than travelers at hotels; but a gentleman who entertained us apologized for his poor table, and
said that it was especially difficult to get good beef, since
Chinamen consider it extravagant to kill such useful animals
as cows and oxen. "Accordingly," he added, "we classify
the so-called
beef that we con-
sume as 'donkey
beef,' 'camel
beef,' and 'preci-
pice beef.'"

THE JINRIKISHA IN CHINA.

"Precipice
beef!" I ex-
claimed, "what in
the world do you
mean by 'preci-
pice beef?'"

"That," he
replied, "is near-
est to the genu-
ine article, for it is the product of a cow that has killed
herself by falling over a precipice."

On one side of this island flows the Canton river, and on
the other is a small canal which separates it from the city.
Two bridges span this narrow stream, each having iron gates
which are invariably closed at night and guarded by sentinels. No Chinese, save employees of the foreigners, may
come within this reservation. In 1883, however, a Chinese
mob attacked it fiercely, and swarmed across the bridges, as
the legendary mice invaded Bishop Hatto's tower on the
Rhine. The English, French, and German families escaped

STARTING FOR CANTON.

to steamers in the river, leaving their houses to be plundered or burned. During my stay here, every evening when this bridge was closed, and every morning when it was reopened, I heard a hideous din of drums and horns, concluding with the firing of a blunderbuss. Our consul told me that the object of all this was to inspire fear. "Tremble and obey!" are the words which close all Government proclamations in the Chinese empire.

The morning after our arrival, we found awaiting us outside the hotel door some coolies with the sedan - chairs in

BRIDGE AT CANTON.

which we were to make our first excursion through Canton.
Another party also was about to start, including several ladies,
each of whom held in her hand either a flask of smelling-salts
or a piece of camphor wrapped in a handkerchief.   In fact,
the druggists of Hong-Kong do quite a business in furnish-
ing visitors to Canton with disinfectants and restoratives.
Some of these ladies feared being insulted by the Canton pop-

A CANTON STREET.

ulace, and told
exciting stories
of an English
lady who had
been recently
spat upon, and
of American
ladies who had
been followed by
a hooting crowd.
Ah Cum, how-
ever, smiled
complacently.
"There is no
danger," he as-
sured us; "my
father will take
care of you la-
dies, as I will of

these gentlemen.   Every one here knows us.   *Our* people
are always safe."

Accordingly we started, crossed the bridge, and two minutes later found ourselves engulfed, like atoms in a sewer, in
the fetid labyrinth of Canton.   One should not be surprised
that illustrations of its streets are not clearer.   The marvel is
that they are visible at all!   "Streets," as we understand
the word, they cannot be truthfully called.   They are dark,

ALONG THE SHORE, CANTON.

tortuous alleys, destitute of sidewalks, and from four to eight feet wide, winding snake-like between long lines of gloomy shops. Comparatively little daylight filters through them to the pavement, not only by reason of their narrow limits, but from the fact that all these passageways are largely filled up, just above the people's heads, with strips of wood, which serve as advertising placards. Many of them are colored blue, red, white, or green, and bear strange characters, gilded or painted on their surfaces. These in the dark perspective of a crowded alley look like the banners of some long procession.

These letters do not give the merchants' names, but serve as trade-marks, like the dedicatory words

TEMPLE OF CONFUCIUS, CANTON.

above the doors of shops in France. How any one can read them is a mystery; not merely on account of the twilight gloom, but from the fact that here at every step one comes in contact with a multitude of repulsive Chinamen, many of them naked to the waist, who seem compressed within this narrow space like a wild torrent in a gorge. To stop in such a place and read a sign appeared to me as difficult as studying the leaves of the trees while riding through a forest on a Texas broncho.

As our bearers pushed their way through these dark,

narrow lanes, the people squeezed themselves against the
walls to let us pass; then closed about us instantly again, like
sharks around the stern of a boat.   At any moment I could

A CANTON COOLIE.

have touched a dozen naked
shoulders with my hand, and
twice as many with my cane.
Meanwhile, to the noise of the
loquacious multitude were
added the vociferations of our
bearers, who shouted constantly
for people to make way, ascrib-
ing to us, we were told, distinguished titles that evidently
excited curiosity even among
the stolid Chinamen.   Occasionally we met a sedan-chair coming in the opposite direction.
Both sets of bearers then began
to yell like maniacs, and we
would finally pass each other

with the utmost difficulty, our coolies having frequently to
back the chair-poles into one shop, and then run them forward into a doorway on the opposite corner, thereby blocking
the noisy, surly crowd until the passage could be cleared.

The faces packed about us, while not positively hostile,
were as a rule unfriendly.   An insolent stare was
characteristic of most of them.   Some disagreeable
criticisms were pronounced, but Ah Cum's
expression never changed, and we, of course,
could not understand them.
Once a banana-skin, thrown
probably by a mischievous
boy, flew by my head; and
I was told that China's

A WHEELBARROW FOR FREIGHT.

favorite exclamation, "foreign devils," was often heard.   But
I dare say that if a Chinese mandarin, in full regalia, were to
walk through some of our streets, he would not fare as well
as we did in Can-
ton; and that if
he ever went to
the Bowery,
"he 'd never go
there any more."

ONE OF THE BROADEST STREETS.

As we kept
passing on
through other
alleys teeming
with half - clad
specimens of the
great unwashed,
I called to mind
the fact that this low class in China has been deliberately
taught to hate, despise, and thoroughly distrust all foreigners.
The unjust opium war with England, the recent territorial
war with France, the stories told them of the treatment of
their countrymen in the United States,—all these would, of

CHINESE TEA-PICKERS.

themselves, be enough to make them hostile; but they are as
nothing to the effect produced upon an ignorant, superstitious
populace by the placards posted on the walls of many Chinese
cities.   I read translations of a few of these, and I believe
they cannot be surpassed in literature for the vulgarity and
infamy of their accusations.   They are in one sense perfectly
absurd; but when we recollect the riotous acts to which they

CHINESE MERCHANTS DRINKING TEA.

have frequently incited their deluded victims, they challenge
serious consideration.

On entering some of the shops that line these passageways, I was astonished at the contrast they presented to the
streets themselves.   The latter are at times no more than
four feet wide.   Not so the shops.   Many of them have a
depth of eighty feet, and in the centre are entirely open to
the roof.   In the corner of each is placed a little shrine.   A
gallery extends around the second story, and on that floor, or

in the rear of the building, the owners live. Some of these shops are handsomely adorned with fine wood-carving and bronze lamps, and on the shelves is stored a great variety of goods, frequently including articles as dissimilar as silk and cotton fabrics, fans, jewelry, umbrellas, Waterbury clocks, and Chinese shoes.

HALL IN A CHINESE HOUSE.

Among these shops we saw a building used partly as a temple and partly as the Guild Hall for the Canton silk merchants. Guilds, or trade-unions, have existed here for centuries. They permeate every branch of

A CHINESE BED AND FURNITURE.

Chinese industry, legal and illegal. Even the thieves form themselves into a guild, and I suppose there is "honor" among them. The origin of these unions is partly due to unjust taxation. Canton contains a vast amount of wealth, but those possessing it are careful to conceal all trace of any superabundance. On this account disputes between the various guilds are settled by arbitra-

tion.   To allow their affairs to go into court would show too
plainly to the tax-collectors their financial status.   Accordingly litigation is almost unknown.   Moreover, when a case
is settled by arbitration, the losing party not only pays the
disputed sum, but is obliged to give a supper to the victor.

In another building that we passed I saw a curious ceremony, which Ah Cum explained as that of three Buddhist
priests who were clearing a house of evil spirits.   It appears

EXORCISING SPIRITS.

that, two weeks before, a
man had committed sui-
cide on the premises, in
order to avenge himself on
the proprietor.   For in
China a man, instead of
killing his enemy, some-
times kills himself, the
motive being a desire that
the hated one shall be regarded as responsible for
his death, and be pursued
by evil spirits here and in
the world to come.   To
be annoyed by ghosts must
be exceedingly unpleasant,
but, on the whole, I hope
that all my enemies will try the Chinese method.

Occasionally we discovered in these streets an itinerant
barber.   These Chinese Figaros carry their outfits with them.
First in importance comes a bamboo pole, which is the immemorial badge of their profession.   To this is usually
attached one solitary towel,—free to every customer.   From
one extremity of this pole hangs a small brass basin, together
with a charcoal stove for heating water; the other end is
balanced by a wooden cabinet, which serves the patient as a

LADY AND MAID.

seat during the operation, and contains razors, lancets, tweezers, files, and other surgical instruments.

It matters not where one of these tonsorial artists prac-
tises his surgery. A temple court, a flight of steps, a street,
or a back-yard, are quite the same to him. He takes his
queue where he can find it. One of his commonest duties is
to braid that customary appendage to a Chinaman's head,

without which he would
be despised. It is com-
ical to estimate the
thousands of miles of
Chinese queues which
even one barber twists
in the course of his
career—enough, if tied
together, end to end,
to form a cable between
Europe and America.
Yet this singular style
of hair-dressing (now
so universal) was in-
troduced into China
only two hundred and
fifty years ago. Before
that time the Chi-

CHINESE BARBER.

nese wore full heads of hair, and the present fashion of
shaved crowns and twisted queues is of Tartar origin, and was
imposed by a conquering dynasty as a badge of servitude.
The wearing of a mustache in China is an indication that he
whose face it adorns is a grandfather. In fact, until he is
forty-five years old, a Chinaman usually shaves his face completely; but this fact does not prove that after that time he
can dispense with the services of a barber. For the tonsorial
art in China is exceedingly varied; and Chinese barbers not

A CHINESE MERCHANT.

only braid the queue; they also shave the eyebrows, clean the ears, pull teeth, and massage. Moreover, they scrape the inside of their victim's eyelids — a custom which is believed by foreigners to be the cause of much of the ophthalmia in China.

Chinese fortune-tellers had for me a singular fascination. I found them everywhere—in temple courts, at gateways and beside the roads—invariably wearing spectacles, and usually seated at a table decorated with huge Chinese characters. Their services seemed to be in great demand. In every case the ceremony was the same. Each applicant in turn approached, and stated what he wished to know; for example, whether a certain day would be a lucky time for him to buy some real estate, or which of several girls his son would better marry. Upon the table stood a tin box full of bamboo sticks. One of these slips the customer drew at random, and from the sentence written on it the fortune-teller gave his answer in oracular words — which could, as usual, be interpreted in various ways.

A CHINESE FORTUNE-TELLER.

A WALL OF CANTON.

At length, however, leaving for a time the shops and dimly - lighted alleys, we found ourselves approaching a huge gate. For Canton, like most other Chinese cities, is divided into certain districts, each of which is separated from the adjoining one by a wall. The gateways in these walls are always closed at night, and are of special use in case of fires or insurrections, since they are strong enough to hold in check a surging crowd till the police or soldiers can arrive.

Passing through this portal, we made our way along the wall until we arrived at a prominent point of observation, known as the Five - storied Pagoda. Whatever this may once have been, it is to-day a shabby, barn-like structure, marked here and there with traces of red paint, like daubs of rouge on a clown's face. All visitors to Canton, however, will recollect the building, with a certain amount of pleasure, as being the resting-place

THE FIVE-STORIED PAGODA.

in which one eats the lunch brought from the steamer or hotel.   Not that there is not food of certain kinds obtainable in Canton itself, but somehow what one sees of Chinese deli- cacies here does not inspire him with a desire to partake of

A WAYSIDE RESTAURANT.

them.   In one of Canton's streets, for example, I entered a cat-restaurant.   Before the door was a notice which Ah Cum translated thus: "Two fine black cats to-day, ready soon." On stepping inside, I heard some pussies mewing piteously in bamboo cages.   Hardly had I entered when a poor old woman brought the proprietor some kittens for sale.   He felt of them to test their plumpness, as we might weigh spring chickens.   Only a small price was offered, as they were very thin, but the bargain was soon concluded, the woman took her money, and the cadaverous kittens went to swell the chorus in the cages.   Black cats, by the way, cost more in China than cats of any other color, for the Chinese believe that the flesh of dark-coated felines makes good blood.

To some Chinamen, dogs fried in oil are also irresistible. In one untidy street, swarming with yellow-skinned humanity, we saw a kind of gipsy kettle hung over a wood fire. Within it was a stew of dog-meat. Upon a pole close by was hung a rump of uncooked dog, with the tail left on, to show the patrons of this open-air restaurant to what particular breed the animal had belonged. For it is said there is a great difference in the flesh of dogs. Bull-terriers, for example, would probably be considered tough. Around this kettle stood a group of coolies, each with a plate and spoon, devouring the canine stew as eagerly as travelers eat sandwiches at a railway restaurant after the warning bell has rung. Some hungry ones were looking on as wistfully as boys outside a bun-shop. One man had such a famished look that, through the medium of Ah Cum, I treated him at once. Moreover, hundreds of rats, dried and hung up by the tails, are exposed for sale in Canton streets, and shark's fins, antique duck eggs, and sea-slugs are considered delicacies.

We tried to bring back photographic proofs of all these horrors, but it was impossible. Whenever we halted in the

CHINAMEN OUT ON A PICNIC.

narrow lanes, in fifteen seconds we would be encircled by a moving wall of hideous faces, whose foremost rank kept closing in on us until the atmosphere grew so oppressive that we gasped for breath and told our bearers to move on. Nor is

this all.   These crowds were sometimes positively hostile.   A
superstitious fear of being photographed by "foreign devils"
made them dangerous.   This fact was several times made dis-

agreeably evi-
dent. Thus, in
a garden adjoin-
ing a Chinese
temple, I wished
to photograph
some "sacred"
hogs which were
attached to the
sanctuary in
some unknown

THE SACRED HOGS.

capacity.   But scarcely had the exposure been made, when a
priest gave the alarm, and in three minutes a mob of men and
boys were rushing toward us, uttering yells and throwing

SORTING TEA.

stones.   Ah Cum himself turned pale.   He sprang in front of
us, and swore (may heaven forgive him!) that not a picture had
been taken.   Of course we offered money as indemnity, but

CHINESE MERCHANTS.

the priests rejected it with scorn, claiming that by the pointing of the camera we had stopped the growth of the hogs.   I do not think I exaggerate the situation when I say that if the politic Ah Cum had not been there to defend us, we should

A CHINESE FARM-HOUSE.

have suffered personal injury.

Standing upon the summit of the Five-storied Pagoda, we looked out over the city of Canton.   For widespread, unrelieved monotony, I never saw the equal of that view in any place inhabited by human beings.   True, the confusion of the foreground was to be excused, since a tornado had recently blown down many of the native houses.   But far beyond this mass of ruins, stretching on and on for miles, was the same monotonous, commonplace vista of low, uninteresting buildings, seamed with mere crevices in lieu of streets. Meantime, from this vast area came to us a dull, persistent hum, like the escape of steam from a locomotive, reminding us that here were swarming nearly two million human beings, almost as difficult for a foreigner to distinguish or identify as ants in a gigantic ant-hill.

THE FLOWERY PAGODA, CANTON.

The exact population of Canton is hard to determine. The number arrived at depends upon where one leaves off counting the three hundred suburban villages, each of which seems a part of the city. Bishop Harper, who lived here for forty years, says, that if one should plant a stake in the centre of Canton, and count all around it within a radius of ten miles, one would find an aggregate of three-and-a-half million people. One village, for example, eleven miles away, noted

for silk and other manufactures, is thought to contain eight hundred thousand inhabitants.

Out of this wilderness of mediocrity there rose in one place a pagoda, which by contrast seemed to possess prodigious height; but such objects are ex-

CANTONESE PAWN-SHOPS.

ceptional. To understand what Canton is like, one must picture to himself a city which, with its suburbs, is larger and more populous than Paris, yet has not one handsome avenue, one spacious square, or even one street that possesses the slightest claim to cleanliness or beauty. Worse than this, it is a city without a single Chinese building in its whole extent that can be even distantly compared in architectural elegance with thousands of imposing structures in any other city of the civilized world. "But are there no European edifices in Canton?" the reader may perhaps inquire. Yes, one, which makes the contrast only more apparent. It is the Roman Catholic cathedral, whose lofty towers are, strangely enough, the first objects in the city which the traveler sees in sailing up the river from Hong-Kong. This handsome Gothic structure, built entirely of granite, rising from such a sea of architectural ugliness, at once called forth our admiration. To the Chinese, however, these graceful towers are objects of the utmost hatred. It angers them to see this area, which French and English conquerors obtained by treaty, still occupied by a Christian church. So far, it has escaped destruction; but there are those who prophesy its doom and say that the time will come when not one stone of it will be left upon another.

There are, however, five or six other buildings in Canton, which rival the pagoda and the Catholic church in height. These hideous objects, which look like monstrous granite boxes set on end, are pawn-shops. One might conclude from their enormous size that half the personal property of the Cantonese was in pawn. They certainly are well patronized, for pawning clothes is such a common thing in China that hundreds of the

CATHOLIC CATHEDRAL, CANTON.

Cantonese send here for safe-keeping their furs and overcoats in summer, and their thin summer clothes in winter, receiving money for them as from any pawn-broker. The Chinese mode of guarding these tall structures against thieves is certainly unique. Upon the roofs are piled stones to be dropped upon the heads of robbers, and also reservoirs of vitriol, with syringes to squirt the horrible acid on invaders.

Astonished at this lack of imposing architecture, we asked

TEMPLE OF FIVE HUNDRED GODS.

if there were no temples in Canton. Assuredly there were— eight hundred of them, all more or less defaced and incrusted with dirt. One of the oldest and most sacred is called the "Temple of Five Hundred. Gods," because within its walls are seated five hundred life-size images of gilded wood, representing deified sages of the Buddhist faith. But they are all coarse specimens of sculpture, and many are amusing caricatures. In front of each is a small jar of ashes, in which the worshiper burns a stick of incense in honor of his favorite god. Offerings of money, too, are sometimes made—but not of genuine money. The Chinese are usually too practical to use anything but imitation money made of gilded paper. I do not know what the gods think of this Oriental style of dropping buttons in the contribution-box, but the priests do not like this sort of currency. They are all "hard money" men.

AN OLD TEMPLE, CANTON.

But, if we accept the ancient proverb that "To labor is to pray," then are the Chinese devout indeed. Whatever other faults they may possess, idleness is not one of them. The struggle for existence keeps them active. Yet they live on almost nothing. A German merchant told me that one

APPROACH TO A SHRINE.

of his coolies, after twenty-five years of service, had recently had his salary raised to ten dollars a month. The laborer was, of course, delighted. "Now," he exclaimed, "I intend to marry another wife. For years I have longed to have two wives, but have never been able to afford it; but now, with ten dollars a month, I can indulge in luxuries!"

In strolling about among these Chinese coolies, I found that life in China is indeed reduced to its lowest terms. In some of the Canton shops, for example, I saw potatoes sold in halves and even in quarters, and poultry is offered, not only singly, but by the piece—so much for a leg, so much for a wing. Second-hand nails are sold in lots of half-a-

ONE OF THE MANY.

dozen. A man can buy one-tenth of a cent's worth of fish or rice. I understood, at last, how Chinese laundrymen can go home from the United States after a few years' work, and live upon their incomes. When one perceives under what conditions these swarming myriads live, one naturally asks how pestilence can be averted. One source of safety is, no doubt, the universal custom of drinking only boiled water in the form of tea. If it were not for this, there would be inevitably a terrible mortality, for the coolies take no precautions against infection. A gentleman in the English consular service told us that he had seen two Canton women in adjoining boats, one washing in the river the bedclothes of her husband who had died of cholera, the other dipping up water in which to cook the family dinner!

If, perchance, these people should fall ill, I fear they would not be greatly benefited by any Chinese doctor whom they might employ. Chinese physicians are thought to be ignoramuses, unless they can diagnose a case by merely feeling the pulse. Hence, if they are called to attend a lady, they see of her usually nothing but her wrist, thrust out between the curtains of the bed. Those who prescribe for internal diseases are called "inside doctors," while others are "outside" men, just as some of our medicines are labeled "for external use only." A story is told of a man who had been shot through the arm with an arrow. He first applied to an "outside" doctor, who cut off the two ends of the weapon and put a plaster on each wound. "But," said the patient, "the remainder of the arrow is still in my arm." "Ah!" replied the "outside" doctor, "that is not my affair. To have that removed, you must go to an 'inside' man."

A CHINESE DOCTOR.

One day, in passing through a temple gate, a half-clad Chinaman offered me for sale a box of grasshoppers, which, when ground into a powder, make a popular remedy for some ailments. In fact, aside from ginseng and a few other well-known herbs, the medicines used in China seem almost incredible. A favorite cure for fever, for example, is a soup of scorpions. Dysentery is treated by running a needle through the tongue. The flesh of rats is supposed to make the hair grow. Dried lizards are recommended as a tonic for "that tired feeling," and

A MEMORIAL GATE.

iron filings are said to be a good astringent. Chinese physicians say that certain diseases are curable only by a decoction whose chief ingredient is a piece of flesh cut from the arm or thigh of the patient's son or daughter. To supply this flesh is thought to be one of the noblest proofs of filial devotion. This is not an exaggeration. In the Pekin *Official Gazette* of July 5, 1870, is an editorial, calling the emperor's attention to a young girl who had cut off two joints of her finger and dropped them into her mother's medicine. The mother recovered, and the governor of the province proposed to erect a monument in honor of the child.

In view of such a pharmacopœia, it is a comfort to learn that in the Chinese theology a

BEGGARS ON THE TEMPLE STEPS.

A CHINESE FUNERAL PROCESSION.

special place in hell is assigned to ignorant physicians. All
quacks are doomed to centuries of torture, the worst fate
being reserved for doctors who abuse their professional skill
for purposes of immorality. Their punishment is the cheerful one of being boiled in oil. Another curious, and not
altogether absurd, custom of the Chinese is to pay a physician
so long as they continue in health, but if they fall ill, the

A GROUP OF CHINESE WOMEN.

doctor's salary ceases until they recover, whereupon it commences again.

Chinese women seemed to me, as a rule, exceedingly
plain, but, even were they Venuses, one of their characteris-
tics would make my flesh creep. I refer to their claw-like
finger-nails, which are so long that apparently they could be
used with equal ease as paper-cutters or stilettoes. Gloves
cannot possibly be worn upon these finger-spikes, so metal
sheaths have been invented to protect them. To show what

LILY FEET.

can be done in nail-growing, the following lengths were measured on the left hand of a Chinese belle: thumb nail, two inches; little finger nail, four inches; third finger, five and one-quarter inches. Under these circumstances we cannot wonder that in China it is not the custom to shake hands: otherwise, painful accidents might occur. Accordingly, the Chinese clasp their own hands and shake them gently at each other.

A still more repulsive peculiarity of Chinese women is their stunted feet, which for the purposes of locomotion are little better than hoofs. All Chinese ladies of the better class must have these "lily feet," as they are called. Sometimes a Chinaman will have two wives; the first an ornamental one with "lily feet," the second, a large-footed woman for business. The origin of this barbarous custom of preventing the growth of the foot is unknown. Perhaps it sprang from a sentiment which Ah Cum graphically expressed by saying: "A small foot is much safer to live with. A big foot runs about too easily and gets into mischief. Moreover," he added, with a

MOTHER AND CHILD

smile, "a big-footed woman sometimes kicks." One Chinaman assured me with great pride that his wife's foot was only
two and a half inches long. There is a class of women here

whose regular business it is
to bind the feet of little
girls when about six years
of age. The process of re-
pressing the natural growth
of the foot lasts for seven
years—the four smaller
toes being bent under
until they lose their
articulations and become
identified with the sole
of the foot. When this
has been accomplished,
the second and severer
operation commences—
of bringing the great toe
and the heel as nearly
together as possible.

A DISTORTED FOOT.

The bandage is drawn
tighter, month by month, until the base of the great toe
is brought into contact with the heel, and the foot has become a shapeless lump. By this unnatural treatment the
leg itself becomes deformed, and its bones are made not
only smaller in diameter, but shorter. The circulation also is
obstructed, and the large muscles are soon completely atro-
phied from disuse. The agony caused by such interference
with nature can be only faintly imagined. It made the tears
come to my eyes to hear a Chinese gentleman describe the
methods taken to console his suffering children and help them
forget their misery. The poor little creatures scream and
moan from the incessant pain, and often lie across the bed

with their legs pressed against the edge, in the hope that this will lessen their distress; but nothing can relieve them but freedom from the torturing bandage, which is never relaxed. It makes one sick at heart to think that such a custom has prevailed in China for more than a thousand years.

Should we approach a group of Chinese merchants in Canton, and ask any one of them "How many children have you?" we could be almost certain that he would not think of

A CHINESE LADY.

counting his daughters, or that he would at least make this distinction—"I have two children, and one girl." For to a Chinaman nothing in life is so important as to have a son to offer sacrifices for him after death and worship at his grave, since, in their opinion, a daughter is not capable of doing this. When a boy is born, therefore, the father is overwhelmed with congratulations, but if the newcomer be a girl, as little reference as possible is made to the misfortune. Friends are informed of the birth of a child by strips of paper carried through the street. If it be a boy, yellow paper is used, but in case of a girl any color will do. This feeling, intensified by poverty, is the cause of the infanticide which has been, and still is, in certain provinces, so dark a blot on the domestic history of China. It is said, for example, that in the vicinity of Amoy thirty per cent. of all new-born girls are strangled or drowned, as unwelcome kittens sometimes are with us.

On our second day in Canton we investigated another

phase of Chinese
life, in some re-
spects stranger
than anything
we had thus far
seen. Along the
shores of the
Canton river, and
in its various ca-
nals, is a popula-
tion of a quarter
of a million souls,

THE HOMES OF THOUSANDS.

living on thousands of peculiar boats crowded together side
by side, and forming streets, and even colonies, of floating
dwellings. Moreover, these conditions prevail in every river-
town throughout the empire.

Each of these "sampans," as they are called, though only
about twenty feet in length, constitutes the home of an entire
family. Eight people frequently live on one boat—grandpa
and grandma, father and mother, uncle and aunt, two or three
children, and a
baby. The lat-
ter is tied to the
back of its moth-
er, even when she
is rowing. As
for the other chil-
dren, their pa-
rents fasten
around them
pieces of bam-
boo, like life-pre-
servers, and tie
them to the rail

A CHINESE PATERFAMILIAS.

by a cord. If they tumble over, they float until some one
gets a chance to pull them in. Upon these little boats thousands are born, eat, drink, cook, and sleep, and finally die,
having known no other home. Under the flooring are stored
their cooking utensils, bedding, clothing, provisions, oil, charcoal, and other requisites of their aquatic life. Above them,

A MARKET-PLACE.

usually, are movable roofs of bamboo wicker-work, to give
protection from the sun and rain.

Some of these families even take boarders! I verified this
by going at night among this floating population, and found
that sleeping space on the boats is rented to those who have no
fixed abode. Planks are laid over the seats to form a floor,
and on these lie the numerous members of the household and

the lodgers. Conspicuous figures in this boat-life are the itinerant barbers and physicians, who go about in tiny *sampans*, ringing a bell and offering their services.

Occasionally, however, we beheld a boat much larger and finer than the craft around it. It proved to be one of the Chinese flower-boats, which are the pleasure resorts of China's *jeunesse dorée*. By day they are conspicuous by their size and gilded wood-work, and in the evening by their many lights. Never, while memory lasts, shall I forget an excursion made at night with our hotel-proprietor among these flower-boats and their surroundings. Many of them were anchored side by side, and planks were stretched from one to the other, like a continuous sidewalk. As we walked along, we passed by countless open doors, each of which revealed a room handsomely furnished with mirrors, marble panels, and blackwood furniture. Here were usually grouped a dozen or more hilarious Chinamen, who were eating, drinking, and smoking, together with professional singing-girls, who are hired by the owners of these flower-boats to entertain their guests with songs and dances. We could not pause to observe them care-

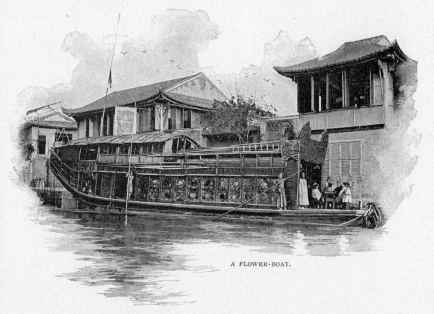

A FLOWER-BOAT.

fully, for foreigners are not wanted here, either as visitors or
patrons.   Meanwhile, at the very doorways of these handsome rooms, beggars in greasy garments crowded around us
and almost threateningly demanded alms.   ''Look out for
your pockets,'' was the proprietor's constant warning.

I have an indistinct remembrance of thus passing row
after row of lighted boats, room after room of painted girls,
group after group of sleek, fat Chinamen at tables, and then,
on leaving these, of seeing miles of loathsome boats contain-

CHINESE MUSICIANS.

ing half-clad men stretched out on bunks and stupefied by
opium, hag-like females cooking over charcoal braziers, and
ragged children huddled in dark corners.   I have a vivid
recollection, too, of walking over slimy planks, of breathing
pestilential odors, and of looking down on patches of repulsive water, so thick with refuse that they resembled in the
lamp-light tanks of cabbage-soup.   We also shudderingly
passed some leper-boats, whose inmates are afflicted with that
terrible disease, and who are forced to live as outcasts, beg-
ging for alms by holding out a little bag suspended from a

bamboo pole.   But finally shaking off the beggars who had
followed us, and fleeing from this multitudinous life, as one
might turn with horror from a pool of wriggling eels, I stag-
gered into the boat belonging to the hotel.   As it moved out
into clearer water, I drew a long breath and looked up at the
stars.   There they were—calm and glorious as ever—scattered in countless numbers through measureless space.   At
any time, when one looks off into the vault of night, our little globe seems insignificant, but never did it seem to me

so tiny and
comparatively
valueless, as
when I left
these myriads
of Chinamen,
swarming like
insects in their
narrow boats,
apparently the
reduction of hu-
manity to the
grade of mi-
crobes.

A TYPICAL CHINESE CRAFT.

The gentle-
man who had accompanied me on this occasion was a Wall
street broker.   "Well," he exclaimed at last, "I have spent
fifteen years among the Bulls and Bears, and I think my
nerves are pretty strong, but for experiences which unnerve
a man, and things which (glad as I am to have seen them
once) I never wish to see again, nothing can compare with
the sights and smells discovered in a trip to Chinatown!"

What impressed me most, however, in this experience was
the idea that the millions in and around Canton are but an
insignificant fraction of the Chinese race.   It filled me with

horror to reflect that all I had witnessed here was but a tiny
sample of the entire empire.   For Canton is said to be superior to many Chinese cities.

One writer has declared that, after walking through the
Chinese quarter of Shanghai, he wanted to be hung on a
clothes-line for a week in a gale of wind.   Tientsin is said to
be still worse for dirt and noxious odors.   Even Pekin, from
all accounts, has horribly paved and filthy thoroughfares,
and its sanitary conditions are almost beyond belief.   If such

A WHEELBARROW BUILT FOR TWO.

then be the state of things in the capital, what must it be in
the interior towns, so rarely reached by foreigners?

It may, however, be objected that in the open ports,
where they encounter foreign influence, the people are at
their worst.   But Chinamen are not impressionable, like the
North American Indians or the aborigines on the islands in the
Pacific, who eagerly adopt the vices of their conquerors, and
speedily succumb to them.

China is one of the oldest countries in the world.   Most of
her ideas, customs, as well as the personal habits of her people

are of immemorial antiquity, and her inhabitants are too conservative to change them. What one beholds in Canton,
therefore, may be fairly supposed to exist from one extremity
of the empire to the other.

But now, among so much that is disagreeable, one naturally
inquires, "Are there not some redeeming features in this Chinese life?" I must confess there are not many discernible
to the passing traveler, but I will gladly mention one about
which I made careful inquiry. It is their honesty in business.
It is the almost invariable custom for Chinese merchants every
New-Year's day to settle their accounts, so that no errors
may be carried over into the coming year; and I was told
that if a tradesman fails to meet his liabilities at that time, he
is considered a defaulter and his credit is forever lost. English and German merchants spoke to us of Chinese commercial honor in the highest terms, and drew comparisons in this
respect between them and the Japanese which were not flat-
tering to the latter.

Even in Japan, I found at all the foreign banks, in some
of the shops, and in the Grand Hotel, that the cashiers were
not Japanese, but Chinamen. Of course, one who has never
traded with them cannot judge of their comparative abilities
in a business way, but merchants in Yokohama, Shanghai,
and Hong-Kong, as well as on the island of Shameen, told
us that Chinamen were more trust-
worthy than the Japanese, and
could be usually depended on to

A MARRIAGE PROCESSION.

live up to their contracts, whether they proved favorable or unfavorable.

An English gentleman who had resided both in China and Japan for years, once said to me: "The more you see of the Japanese the less you will like them. The more you see of the Chinese the less you will dis-like them. You will always like the Japanese; you will always dislike Chinamen; but the degree in which you cherish and express these senti-ments will constantly diminish."

A CHINESE JUNK.

Besides the numerous differences between Oriental and Occidental customs noticed in Japan, we found in China many other proofs of what has been well called a state of topsy-turvydom. Thus, our tail-ors draw the needle inward; Chinese tailors stitch outward. With us mili-tary men wear their swords on the left side; in China they are worn on the right. In boxing the compass a Chinaman says "East, West, South, North." To mark a place in a book we turn the corner of a page inside; a Chinaman bends it the other way. We print the title of a volume on the back; the Chinese on the front. We play battledore and shuttlecock with our hands; the Chinese use their feet for a battledore and catch the shut-tlecock on their foreheads. We use our own names when engaged in business; in China fancy names are taken. We carry one watch hidden in our pocket; a Chinese gentleman sometimes wears two outside his clothes, with their faces exposed. We black our boots; the Chinese whiten theirs. With us it is considered impolite to ask a person's age; in China it is a high compliment, and there a man is congratulated if he

SACRED ROCKS, INTERIOR OF CHINA.

is old. Men, at least in the Occident, have plenty of pockets; the Chinaman has none, and uses his stockings as receptacles

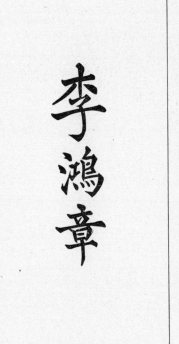

LI HUNG CHANG'S VISITING-CARD.

for papers, and at the back of his neck inserts his folded fan. At our weddings youthful bridesmaids are desired; at Chinese nuptials old women serve in that capacity. We launch our vessels lengthwise; the Chinese launch theirs sidewise. We mount a horse from the left; they mount their horses from the right. We begin dinner with soup and fish, and end with dessert; they do exactly the reverse. Finally, the spoken language of China is never written, and the written language is never spoken.

After all, however, we should remember that Chinamen who travel in our own country think that our customs are as strange as theirs appear to us. A prominent official of the Flowery Kingdom, who made the tour of Europe several years ago, took notes of what he saw, and published them on his return. Among them are the following: "Women, when going to the drawing-room of Queen Victoria regard a bare skin as a mark of respect." "When people meet and wish to show affection, they put their lips and chins together and

A JOSS-HOUSE.

make a smacking sound." This is not so difficult to understand, when we recollect that, like most Orientals, the Chinese do not kiss, and that even a mother does not kiss her own baby, although she will press it to her cheek. Again, he thus describes our dancing parties: "A European skipping match is a strange sight. To this a number of men and women come in couples, and enter a spacious hall; there, at the sound of music, they grasp each other by both arms, and leap and prance backward and forward, and round and round,

WATERING-PLACE FOR ANIMALS.

till they are forced to stop for want of breath. All this," he adds, "is most extraordinary;" and when we Occidentals think of it, perhaps it is. A Chinese youth, after eating for the first time a European dinner, wrote of his experience: "Dishes of half-raw meat were served, from which pieces were cut with sword-like instruments and placed before the guests. Finally came a green and white substance, the smell of which was overpowering. This, I was informed, was a compound

PLACE OF EXECUTION, CANTON.

of sour milk, baked in the sun, under whose influence it remains until it becomes filled with insects; yet the greener and livelier it is, the greater the relish with which it is eaten! This is called *Che-sze.*"

The object of most gruesome interest to me in Canton was its place of execution. On entering this, I looked about me with astonishment; for almost all the space between the rough brick walls was filled with coarse, cheap articles of pottery. Ah Cum explained, however, that when a batch of heads are to be cut off, the jars are all removed, much as a hotel

A PAGODA.

dining-room is cleared for dancing. The condemned prisoners are always brought in baskets to this place, and are compelled to kneel down with their hands tied behind their backs. Their queues are then thrown forward, and they are beheaded at a single stroke. Traces of blood were visible on the ground, and from a mass of rubbish close at hand a grinning Chinaman pulled out several skulls which he had hidden there, and claimed a fee for exhibiting them. I was presented to the executioner, and asked him how many men he had himself decapitated, but he could not tell. He kept no count, he said—some days six, some days ten, in all probably more than a thousand. As he was resolutely opposed to having his picture taken, we placed his two-edged sword against the wall, and photographed that. When I was told that, once a week, twenty or thirty men are brought into this filthy court to die like cattle in a slaughter-house, I stood aghast, but when I subsequently learned that this is the only execution-place in a great province with a population of twenty

DRAWING WATER.

FEMALE CULPRITS.

millions, the number did not seem so appallingly excessive. This is, however, merely the average in ordinary times. After certain insurrections, such as the Taiping rebellion, this hideous square has seemed almost a reservoir of human blood. The venerable missionary, Dr. Williams, states that he saw here one morning at least two hundred headless trunks, and stacks of human heads piled six feet high. Careful estimates place the number executed here during fourteen months, at eighty-one thousand,— or more than thirteen hundred every week!

I doubt if many criminals beheaded here feel much regret at leaving life, so horrible has been their previous condition in the Canton prison. We visited this institution, but to obtain a picture of it was impossible. Within an ill-kept, loathsome area, we saw a crowd of prisoners wearing chains, while around their necks were heavy wooden collars, which, being from three to five

A PRISONER.

feet square, were so wide that the poor wretches wearing
them could never possibly feed themselves, but must depend
on others for their nourishment. How they lie down to sleep
with them on I do not know. Yet they must wear such collars

JUDGE AND PRISONERS.

for weeks, and
even months, at
a time. I have
no sentimental
sympathy for
criminals, and
thoroughly be-
lieve in the en-
forcement of just
laws, but I was
shocked at the
sight of these
poor creatures. Whatever may have been their guilt, such
treatment is a degradation of humanity.

Leaving the place of execution, we made our way to one
of the criminal courts of Canton. It was in session when we
entered it, and I never can forget the sight that met my gaze.
Before the judge was a prisoner on his knees, pleading for
mercy and protesting innocence. Chains were around his
neck, waist, wrists, and ankles. Beside him knelt an aged
woman, whose gray hair swept the floor as she rocked back
and forth, imploring vengeance on her son's assassin. At
last the culprit confessed his crime of murder, and was led
back to prison. How sincere his confession was, it would be
hard to say; for if, in the face of powerful adverse testimony,
an accused man still asserts his innocence, he is often pun-
ished in the court-room till he does confess. Around the hall
were various instruments of torture—bamboo rods to flog the
naked back; hard leather straps with which to strike the prisoner on the mouth, thus sometimes breaking the teeth and

even the jaw; thumb-screws and cords by which he is suspended by his thumbs and toes; and heavy sticks with which
to beat his ankles. I did not happen to see these used,
because in the three trials I witnessed all of the prisoners
confessed. But they are used; and just as I was entering the
court, I met a criminal being led back to prison, so weak and
crippled by his punishment, that he could hardly step without assistance. Curiously enough, after the torture has been
administered, the culprit is required to fall upon his knees
and thank the judge. This I should think would be "the
most unkindest cut of all."

It seems impossible to say anything in defense of such a
system as this; for in China a man is not only looked upon as

guilty till he is
proved innocent,
but is kept in
loathsome con-
finement, and
may be even put
upon the rack, in
spite of the es-
tablished fact
that torture is
never a test of
truth. And yet
a foreign resident
made, as an apol-
ogy, the follow-
ing statement:
"You must re-

A CHINESE COURT.

member that testimony here amounts to nothing, and that,
by paying sixpence apiece, you can pack the court-room with
men who will swear that black is white. Hence, where a man
can easily bribe false witnesses to ruin his enemy, the Chinese

law provides that no one shall under any circumstances be
put to death unless he has confessed his crime.   But since a
prisoner on trial for his life will usually protest his innocence
to the last, the court attempts by torture to force him to
confess.''

We visited finally an object in Canton far pleasanter than
its scenes of punishment, yet equally characteristic of the
national life.   It is the place where natives of this province
take the first step in the only path which in China leads to
political and social rank.   It is the scene of the competitive
examinations, the fame of which has filled the world.

THE EXAMINATION GROUND, CANTON.

The courtyard where the contest takes place is by no means
inviting.   It is an area of sixteen acres, covered with nearly
nine thousand rough brick sheds.   At the time of an examination each of these is occupied by a candidate.   Before he
enters it, his person is carefully searched, and soldiers and
policemen guard all passageways to prevent communication.
"Each in his narrow cell," these applicants for office then
remain for three consecutive days and nights, about as pleas-
antly lodged, I should imagine, as Jonah was for the same
length of time; for these dirty dens of brick are only four
feet long, three feet wide, and possibly six feet high.   One
of the horse-sheds in the rear of a New England meeting-

THE GREAT WALL AT A PRECIPICE.

house would be a far more comfortable place in which to eat and sleep. Perhaps they are meant, however, to emphasize the triumph of mind over matter. Their only furniture consists of two small planks, one for a seat, the other for a table. Rest is, of course, impossible in such a cage, and candidates have sometimes died here from physical and mental strain. All this seems inexcusably cruel; yet the Chinese government may have good reasons for maintaining this severity. For instance, such a system, if intro-

A STUDENT.

duced at Washington, would rid the District of Columbia of nine-tenths of its office-seekers within twenty-four hours. While some of these students persevere in their attempts till they are seventy or eighty years of age, others are quite young; but the fact of youth is not considered discreditable, for Confucius said: "A youth should always be regarded with respect. How do we know that his future may not be superior to our present?" At all events, the highest place is

FISHING ON THE RIVER.

open to them, if their brains will take them there; for every village in China has its school, and every free-born citizen may qualify for this struggle, the governing principle of

which is "Let the best man win!"   It is the law of the "sur-
vival of the fittest" exemplified in politics.

In all the provinces of China, on the appointed day, thousands of candidates assemble, eager for the contest.   Subjects
are given them on which they must produce a poem and original essays.   Their work is then examined by officials ap-

A CHINESE GENERAL AND HIS ATTENDANTS.

pointed by the Government, and so extremely rigid is the
test, that out of every thousand applicants only about ten
gain the first, or "District," degree.   There are, however,
three degrees to be attained by Chinese aspirants for fame.
Those who come out as victors in the first receive no office,
but are at least exempt from corporal punishment, and may
attempt the examination for the next degree.   Even the few
who pass the second, or "Provincial," test (about one in a

hundred) receive no government appointment. Yet they
are distinguished among their countrymen by wearing a gold
button in their hats, and by a sign over their houses signifying
"Promoted man."

Those who succeed in standing the third, or "Imperial,"
test at Pekin,—severer even than the other two,—have reached
the apex of the pyramid. They
are now mandarins, and have
acquired all they can desire,—
social distinction, office, wealth,
and (what is sometimes still
more highly prized) great national fame. For in the results
of this examination the entire
country takes the greatest interest. The names of the successful men are everywhere
proclaimed by means of couriers, river-boats, and carrier-
pigeons, since thousands of
people in the empire have laid
their wagers on the candidates,
as we might do on horses at the
Derby. Strange, is it not, to
think that this elaborate Chinese system was practised in

LI HUNG CHANG.

the land of the Mongols substantially as it is to-day, at a time
when England was inhabited by painted savages?

Moreover, the honors of successful candidates in China
cannot be inherited. Young men, if they would be ennobled,
must surpass their competitors and win their places as their
fathers did. Even the youthful son of Li Hung Chang, whom
General Grant considered, next to Bismarck, the most remarkable man he met with in his tour around the world, is

not entitled, because of his father's office, to any special rank. Hence, China, though an absolute monarchy, has no privileged class whose claims rest merely on the accident of birth. Her aristocracy consists of those who have repeatedly proved themselves intellectually superior to their rivals. Among no people in the world, therefore, have literary men received such honors as in China; and it is a remarkable fact that this vast nation has worshiped for two thousand years, not a great

LI HUNG CHANG AND SUITE ON THEIR TOUR AROUND THE WORLD.

warrior, nor even a prophet claiming inspiration from God, but a philosopher,—Confucius.

I have often thought that were I asked to compare the Chinese empire of to-day with some material object, I would select for such comparison the Great Wall on its northern frontier. This mighty work has hardly been surpassed in the whole history of architecture, not even by the builders of the Pyramids. It is no less than twenty-five feet high and forty feet broad, with watch-towers higher still, at intervals of three hundred feet. And yet it has a length of nearly fifteen hundred miles, a distance exceeding that from Boston to St. Paul, and in its uninterrupted march spans deep ravines and climbs to lofty mountain crests, in one place nearly five thousand feet in height. Although it was built three hundred years before the birth of Christ, it still exists, and during fourteen

THE GREAT WALL OF CHINA.

centuries sufficed to hold in check the savage tribes of Tartars from the north. It has been calculated that if the Great Wall were constructed at the present time, and with Caucasian labor, its cost would pay for all the railroads in the United States. One hundred years ago an English engineer reckoned that its masonry represented more than all the dwellings of England and Scotland put together, and, finally, that its material would construct a stone wall six feet high and two feet thick around the entire globe.

In many respects this great rampart is typical of China. Both have a vast antiquity, both have an enormous extent, and both have had their periods of glory, — China her age of progress and invention, and this old wall a time when it was kept in perfect order, when warriors stood at every tower, and when it stretched for

A GATEWAY IN THE GREAT WALL.

fifteen hundred miles—an insurmountable barrier to invasion. But just as this leviathan of masonry has outlived its usefulness, and is at present crumbling to decay, so the huge Chinese empire itself now seems decrepit and wholly alien to the nineteenth century. Her roads, once finely kept, are now disgraceful; her streets are an abomination to the senses; her rivers and canals are left to choke themselves through want of dredging; and even her temples show few signs of care. Stagnation and neglect are steadily at work on her colossal frame, as weeds and plants disintegrate this mouldering wall. Will this old empire ever be aroused to new activity, and can fresh life-blood be infused into her shrunken veins to animate her inert frame? There is, I think, a possibility that, in the coming century, the new, progressive party here will overcome the dull conservatism of the nation, connect her vast interior with the sea, utilize her mineral wealth, develop her immense resources, and make her one of the great powers of the world. Napoleon once warned England that if the Chinese should learn too well from her the art of war, and then acquire the thirst for conquest which has characterized other nations, the result might be appalling to the whole of Europe. For think what inexhaustible armies they could raise, and what great fleets they could build and launch upon their mighty rivers! But this is a problem of the future, about which no man can predict with certainty.

Many have asked me if I am glad that I went to China, and I have always answered that, as a unique and useful study of humanity, I think it one of the most valuable experiences of my life. Still I am bound to say, that when I stood upon the deck of an outgoing steamer, and felt it move beneath my feet responsive to the engine's stroke, I drew a breath of pleasure and relief. For I was assured that the

A LEVIATHAN OF MASONRY.

swarming millions of the Chinese empire were being left
behind me, and that my face was turned toward that historic
land where, lighted by the Southern Cross, I was to visit
Hindu shrines and Mogul palaces, and gaze on the Himalayas
and the Taj Mahal.